Paper Crafting
with
Carol Duvall™

This book is lovingly dedicated to my viewers.

You have been loyal, helpful, understanding, patient and supportive.
You have amazed me with your talent and delighted me with your sense of humor.
I admire your eagerness to learn and your willingness to try new things.
I appreciate your generosity in sharing your ideas and your accomplishments.

Without you my career would have not have been … and I thank you.

Paper Crafting with Carol Duvall

Copyright © 2007 DRG, 306 East Parr Road, Berne, Indiana 46711

EXECUTIVE EDITOR	Jeanne Stauffer
EDITOR	Tanya Fox
ART DIRECTOR	Brad Snow
PUBLISHING SERVICES DIRECTOR	Brenda Gallmeyer
ASSOCIATE EDITOR	Sue Reeves
ASSISTANT ART DIRECTOR	Nick Pierce
COPY SUPERVISOR	Michelle Beck
COPY EDITOR	Mary O'Donnell
TECHNICAL EDITORS	Marla Freeman, Brooke Smith
GRAPHIC ARTS SUPERVISOR	Ronda Bechinski
GRAPHIC ARTIST	Amy S. Lin
PRODUCTION ASSISTANTS	Erin Augsburger Marj Morgan Judy Neuenschwander
PHOTOGRAPHY SUPERVISOR	Tammy Christian
PHOTOGRAPHY	Don Clark, Matthew Owen, Jackie Schaffel
PHOTO STYLISTS	Tammy Nussbaum, Tammy M. Smith
CHIEF EXECUTIVE OFFICER	David J. McKee
BOOK MARKETING DIRECTOR	Dwight Seward
MARKETING VICE PRESIDENT	Dan Fink

Printed in China
First Printing: 2007
Softcover ISBN: 978-1-59635-142-4
Hardcover ISBN: 978-159635-141-7
Library of Congress Number: 2007924954

CONTENTS

Creative Cards

7

Chalk Talk 9
Woven Paper Cards 12
Long & Lean Letter Cards ... 16
Bleach Party 21
Red Hearts Pop-up Card 24
Stamped Pop-up Card.......... 27
Illustrated Pop-up Cards 30
Two-for-One Cards.............. 32
Hearts Galore Cards............. 35
Illuminated Letters 37
"Leftovers" Cards 41
Scrapbook Paper Cards & Envelopes.......................... 44
Paper Napkin Cards 49

Just Because

53

Pop-up Packages 54
Poof Maker 59
Little Boxes 62
Paper Flower Napkin Rings 68
One-Sheet Mini Books 70
Dodecahedron Mobile............ 75
Fold-up Gift Boxes 80
Pretty Pillow Boxes................ 83
Mizuhiki Decorated Boxes 88
Match the Cutouts 92

All materials provided in this book by or on behalf of HGTV or otherwise associated with HGTV's program *The Carol Duvall Show* are owned by Scripps Networks Inc. and are used under license by DRG Publishing. "HGTV," "Home and Garden Television," the HGTV logo, and the title *The Carol Duvall Show* are service marks and/or trademarks of Scripps Networks Inc.

HGTV inspires and empowers people to imagine, create and enjoy where they live. Its wide variety of programming is a combination of entertaining stories, helpful information and insights from hosts who are recognized experts in their fields. Moving beyond four walls and a roof, and tapping into the emotional connections people have with the place they call home, HGTV is the best place for them to start making a life they love. Viewers can find even more of what they love about HGTV at HGTV.com, with thousands of photos and decorating ideas, interactive design tools, easy-to-make projects, videos and more. Now in more than 91 million homes, HGTV is part of the Scripps Networks portfolio of lifestyle oriented cable networks including Food Network, DIY Network, FINE LIVING TV NETWORK and Great American Country (GAC).

All of us at DRG Publishing are dedicated to providing you with innovative information and ideas. We welcome your comments and suggestions. Write to us at: DRG, Editorial Department, 306 East Parr Road, Berne, IN 46711.

If you would like to purchase any of our books, check wherever quality books are sold. Or visit us at: DRGbooks.com.

2 3 4 5 6 7 8 9 10

Paper Plus

95

Rock, Paper, Scissors 96

Changeable Place Mats 98

Coffee-Filter Flowers 101

Chalk Marbleized Paper 104

Quotes—Famous &
  Otherwise 107

Clock in a Bag 111

Refrigerator Puzzles 115

Note Card Coasters 119

Show-Offs

123

Never-Ending Card 124

Stamp & Fold Frames 128

Look Who's Talking 131

Greeting Card Frames 132

Pictured-Topped Shaker
  Boxes........................... 135

Personality Frames 137

Jacob's Ladder
  Photo Folder................... 140

Art in Miniature 144

From the Shoe Box

147

Mosaic Photo Cards 149

Crafting With Envelope
  Linings........................... 153

ABC Book 155

Punched Paper Petals 156

A Locking Letter................. 158

Bag 'Em..............................162

Desktop Calendar................164

Molded Tissue Cards 167

Buyer's Guide...................... 174

Hello!

Welcome to my world of paper crafting. I'm delighted that you have picked up this book, and I hope that you will read it, enjoy it, and even better, make something from it. It has been a long time in coming—a very long time, but not to worry. You've not missed a thing. I've saved many of the ideas that have been your favorites and mine over the years and have included them in the following pages. Many have been redone in more modern dress; some are much the same as they were then; others are basically the same projects but are made a little differently (we didn't have all the punches, personal die-cut machines and Xyron machines at the time). And of course, there are many projects that I hope will be brand-new to you.

I have already realized that the title of this book begs the question: With the variety of crafting I have done over the years, how did I come to pick paper as the focal point of this book? For starters, paper is probably the hottest single product in the craft world today, which means that a lot of you are as fascinated with it as I am, and for me, it was a natural because paper is where it all started.

It was paper that was my first crafting medium, though at the time the word "crafting" wasn't even in my vocabulary. We called it "making things," and paper was there to make things with.

There was construction paper, school paper, crepe paper, tissue paper and newspaper. It was readily available and easy to glue. It could be cut or torn, folded or woven, and painted or colored with crayons to make beads, belts, bracelets, "cootie catchers," paper chains and drinking cups, and you could write on it. You can still do all those things, of course, but with the paper we have today, even the simplest little project can be a thing of beauty. So paper it is!

With me every step of the way through all the cutting, folding, stamping and gluing for this book has been my good friend Cherryl Greene. Those of you who have been long-time viewers of *The Carol Duvall Show*, already know Cherryl as an enthusiastic crafter, a stamper who would probably mortgage her house for another rubber stamp and the producer who keeps me on track. She is organized enough for both of us. She has worked with me since day one of this book. She has done some of the projects. I have done others. Some we have worked on together. Sometimes I will get the idea, and she will execute it. Other times we will each do our version of the same project. We worked hard and enjoyed it all because we were both doing what we love to do … craft. I can only hope that the enthusiasm and the pleasure are contagious.

Enjoy!

Carol

Creative Cards

It was rather recently that I got into card making and I love it! Not that I didn't experiment with it some years ago, but at that time it was a major production just to get the materials for making the basic cards, much less decorating them. Now there's a whole world of wonderful supplies out there, and you can go from start to finish in an hour. You can make them pop up or fold up or spin. You can stamp them, add photos or write a personal note inside. It's no wonder that card making has become such a favorite with crafters. So has card receiving. In a world where most written communication is done via e-mail, there's nothing like the personal touch of receiving a handmade card. When you're a card maker, everybody benefits.

Chalk Talk

This is an intriguing way to make unusual note cards using chalk as your color source, and your finger or a chenille pompom as your tool of choice for applying the color. Bring this old technique up to date using punches and rubber stamps, and of course, your creativity.

Materials

Matte-finish note cards
 with envelopes
Colored chalks
White paper or
 card stock
Rubber stamps
Alphabet stickers
Die-cut machine
Small pompoms
Spray fixative (optional)

1 Cut a strip of paper or card stock about 4 inches wide. Use a chalk stick to color a strip about 1½ inches wide along one long edge. Repeat with several other colors and strips of paper.

Note

If desired, you can spray the completed cards with a fixative although I have never found it necessary.

2 Tear along the colored edge to make a rough edge. Tear away from you and not toward you so the color comes all the way to the torn edge. Repeat with the other strips of paper.

3 Place the torn edge on top of the note card. With your finger or pompom, brush the chalk onto the note card along the full length of the card.

4 Move the torn paper down ½ inch or so and repeat the process, or use another strip of paper with another color. Repeat this process with the same color or many colors until the card is covered. ∎

A brushed chalk background and rubber-stamped pieces that have been chalked and adhered to square cutouts create an interesting card design.

Brushed chalk was used to color the frog and to make the checked background.

Variations

Place the colored strip a measured distance from the edge of the paper to make a border. Do this along all four edges. You can do this with a straight edge instead of a torn one, or use decorative scissors to cut the edge.

With small scissors, large punches or a die-cutting machine, cut out shapes like hearts, circles or diamonds, and use as stencils when making cards.

Woven Paper Cards

Those who bring sunshine
to the lives of others
cannot keep it from themselves

It was Debra Anderson of Custer's Last Stamp who showed me how to make these, and I found them to be fascinating. Though they are basically just stamped and embossed cards, the weaving gives them a whole new look. Whether you stamp and then emboss, or emboss and then stamp depends on the look you prefer. I prefer to stamp and then emboss, but try both ways.

Materials

Card stock cut into ¼-inch-wide strips	Tweezers
	Heat gun
Clear pigment ink pad (for embossing)	Cutting mat with measured grid
Permanent ink pad (for stamped image)	Craft knife and ruler, or paper cutter
Dye-based ink pad (for background color)	Double-sided tape
Rubber stamp	
Regular clear embossing powder	
Optional: ultra-thick gold embossing powder	

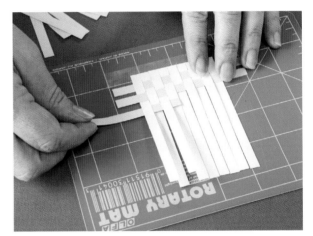

1 Place a strip of double-sided tape along a horizontal line on the cutting-mat grid. Lay down one of the cut card-stock strips, positioning it at a right angle to the tape and placing it so it overlaps the bottom edge of the tape approximately ¼ inch, making sure it is perfectly straight. Place a second card-stock strip next to the first one, butting the two together. Repeat with as many strips as it takes to make the desired width. ***Note:** The size of the woven piece will be determined by the size of the stamped image you select. Our initial woven piece measured 4 inches, using 4-inch-long strips to accommodate our 2¼ x 3¼-inch butterfly image. The stamped piece was later trimmed slightly in width and length. We are using two different-colored strips for the photo only.*

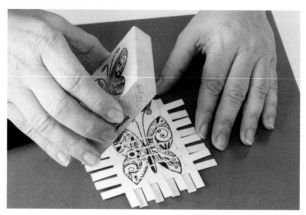

2 Weave the remaining card-stock strips through the vertical strips in a basket-weave pattern until you have a piece of desired size. Carefully remove the woven piece from the tape and place on work surface.

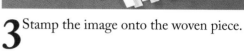

3 Stamp the image onto the woven piece.

4 Add some color by swiping the dye-based ink pad across the surface.

5 Cover the entire surface of the woven piece with clear pigment ink by dabbing the surface with the ink pad.

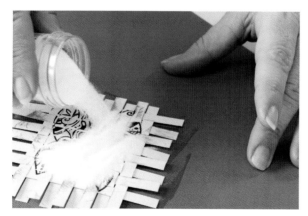

6 Apply a generous layer of regular clear embossing powder to the inked surface.

7 Pick up the woven piece with tweezers and shake off the excess powder.

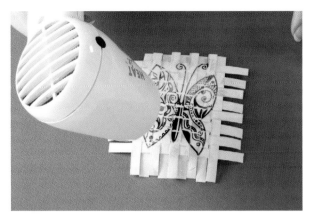

Tip

You can continue to build up layers of regular embossing powder by sprinkling the powder over the surface while the melted powder is still hot. It doesn't get as thick as using ultra-thick enamel, but it is very effective.

8 Heat with the heat gun until powder is melted. Repeat if desired. ∎

Variation

If you prefer to emboss and then stamp, you will need to use the ultra-thick embossing enamel instead of regular embossing powder.

1 Ink the stamp first with permanent ink and set it aside, rubber side up. *Note: If an impression of the stamp is preferred rather than a colored image, ink*

the stamp with clear pigment ink. Cover the surface of the woven piece with clear pigment ink, and holding it with tweezers, dip it into the gold ultra-thick embossing powder. Heat with heat gun; immediately reapply the embossing powder and heat again. Repeat one or two more times.

2 While the embossing powder is still hot, press the pre-inked stamp into it. Impress firmly and let the stamp remain there for just a minute, or until the hot, melted powder begins to cool.

3 When the piece has cooled, lift the stamp. Attach the finished woven piece to the front of a card, a small bag or a small gift package, or adhere a pin back to it and wear it as a pin.

Long & Lean Letter Cards

Any kind of fool-the-eye puzzles or illusions intrigue me, and I've been fascinated with these mysterious-looking letters since my father taught me the technique for drawing them when I was 9 years old. I used a pencil and ruler back then and spent an inordinate amount of time just printing out the names of everyone I knew.

Now with our computers and printers, we can "draw" these long, tall letters in minutes to use for personalizing unique notes and stationery, and still keep the illusion.

Materials

Handmade or purchased card
Card stock for printing letters
Computer and printer

Mystery Solved

To read the letters on the opposite page hold the book at an angle facing away from you. For the horizontally printed letters turn the book sideways and angle down.

The Card

1 The basic card can either be made by hand or purchased. The size and shape of the card will help determine the size and shape of the area required for the letters.

2 Generate the letters on your computer, print, cut out and glue onto card blank. You can also enter the measurements for the card, size the letters accordingly and print them directly on the cards in any colors you wish. In either case we leave the design and construction of the cards up to you. You can use your decorative-edged scissors for cutting. Attach the cut-out letters with brads or sticky dots or a glue stick. Add glitter and put everything on patterned paper. There are many choices. The design and construction of the cards are up to you. But *first*, the letters.

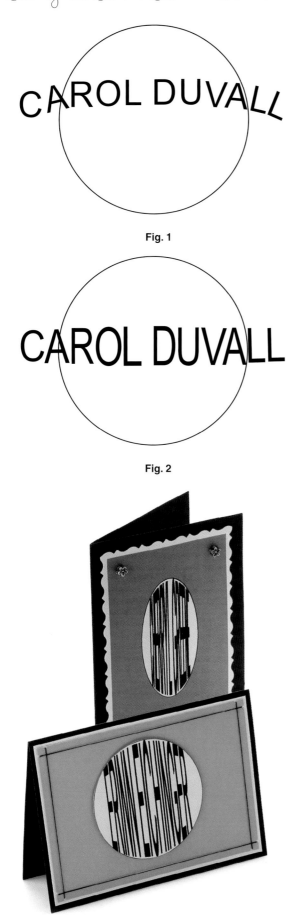

Fig. 1

Fig. 2

Creating the Letters

1 Whether you use a PC or a Mac, the programs you need will be there. You just have to find them. For those of you who are familiar with your computer and what it will do, you can pretty much ignore the following. For those of you who are still in the hunt-and-experiment stage, the following might be of help in getting you there. I used a PC with Windows XP.

2 In **Microsoft Word**, I went to **View** then down to **Toolbars** and clicked on **Drawing** and **WordArt**. In the **Drawing** toolbar, I clicked on the outline of an oval. When you click on it, a drawing area outlined by a rectangle will appear. Click inside this area then click and drag on the tiny circles that appear to make your circle. Enlarge it to the desired size. Click on **Word Art** (the tilted capital A on the toolbar) and select one of the squares. I selected the words that used very plain, black letters. Click on **OK**. When the **Edit** box appears, select a font. It should be plain, not bold and contain no serifs. I selected **Arial** and 36-point, but if you have a very long name, use a lower number. It makes no difference in the finished item, but it will be easier to work with. Type desired uppercase letters/words. Click on **OK**.

3 The words you have typed will appear in the circle, but not in a compatible shape (Fig. 1). Select **Abc** in the toolbar and select the shape that is curved along the top and the bottom. It is called "inflate."

4 The letters print out slightly taller in the middle than they are on the ends (Fig. 2), but as you click on the various dots that appear, you will be able to manipulate the letters so that they fit in the circle (Fig. 3). My name is very short so the letters are very legible. You might prefer them this way. If not, just keep pushing the sides in using the dots to move them. Of course, if my name were longer (Mary Margaret Duvall) it would look like Fig. 4. Or you might just prefer to skip the whole idea of a circle and print yours in a straight line (Fig. 5).

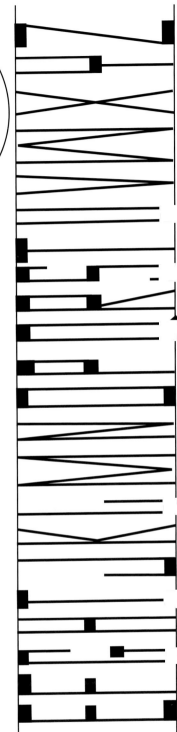

Long & Lean Letter Hand-Printed Alphabet

Fig. 3

Fig. 4

5 Either select a background design and/or color on the computer and print out your letters on white card stock; or select whatever card stock you want for the background and print your circle of letters on that. Cut it out and adhere to your selected card, or print out the entire card on the computer selecting both the background for the card itself as well as for the letters in the circle. ■

Fig. 5

Note

To read what is printed hold the card at an angle in front of you angling it away from you. The longer and leaner the letters the more of an angle required.

Tip

To really do things the handmade way, copy our alphabet using a ruler and fine-line pen for drawing the letters. Working upside down and staying between the lines, print the letters right to left so the ruler doesn't cover your work. Keep making the letters longer and leaner and closer together until you can't read them straight on. Then curve some of the round letters (see B, C and D) if you wish.

Bleach Party

This was great fun because it involved so much experimentation. I achieved a variety of results, depending on the kind of paper or card stock I used. With some card stock, nothing happened. In other cases, the changes were almost instantaneous. The same held true with the kind of product used. Thick, liquid dishwasher detergent sometimes resulted in a different look from that obtained when using straight liquid laundry bleach. By trying different products, you can discover some interesting and surprising effects. You never know what colors you will get.

Materials

Large plastic bag to cover tabletop

Dark-colored construction paper and/or card stock

Liquid household bleach

Liquid dishwasher detergent

Disposable plastic foam tray

Several layers of paper towel, or a piece of white felt for "ink pad"

Foam brush

Rubber stamps, spritzer bottle, soft-bristled old brushes, cotton swabs, etc.

Glue or tape

Project notes: Other than colored card stock or paper and bleach, the items listed are optional. You may substitute where needed. Those listed are what I used.

When using the liquid household bleach, it best to use the plastic bag to protect the tabletop from stray squirts of the bleach. Put some in a spritzer bottle and spray different-colored papers and/or card stock. That's all. These pieces can be used for background patterns or punched into smaller accent pieces with a paper punch.

When using the dishwasher detergent with rubber stamps, use a foam brush to apply the detergent

Samples of spritzed papers

sparingly to the stamp. Stamp the paper. In some cases the fading will happen almost immediately. In other cases it may take several minutes.

When using liquid household bleach with rubber stamps, make an ink pad by placing a piece of white felt or several layers of paper toweling in a foam meat tray. Press the rubber stamp to the pad and stamp the paper as if you were stamping with ink.

Try using an old paintbrush with soft bristles to apply the bleach or detergent to the paper. Different brushes will give you different effects.

Stamp and emboss a design on a piece of paper or card stock, then apply the bleach or detergent to portions of the stamped image using a cotton swab or paintbrush. (See the Believe card on page 20.)

Dishwasher detergent or bleach ... which is which? Use what you have or experiment with both.

Making Cards

1 Cut one 8½ x 11-inch piece of card stock in half crosswise. Fold one of these pieces in half vertically to form a 4¼ x 5½-inch side-fold card.

2 Cut the remaining half sheet of card stock into two 4¼ x 5½-inch pieces. Brush one piece vertically with bleach or detergent using an old paintbrush and let dry. Place this faded piece on top of the front of your card and attach with glue or tape. *Note: To frame the bleached panel with the original card-stock color, trim ½ inch from two adjacent sides of the bleached panel, then center and adhere to the card front.*

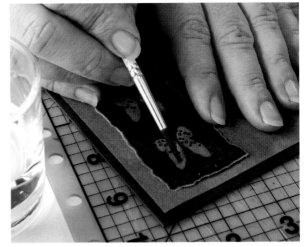

3 Stamp a design on the remaining piece of card stock using a dark ink and embossing powder. Tear around the edges of the design. If you tear toward you, a portion of the underneath side will be visible. Brush this with the detergent or bleach to highlight the design. Attach to the card with glue or tape.

4 "Color in" any desired parts of the design using a paintbrush or cotton swab dipped in bleach or detergent. Add any desired embellishments such as a button or bow. See completed card in photo on page 20. ∎

Red Hearts Pop-up Card

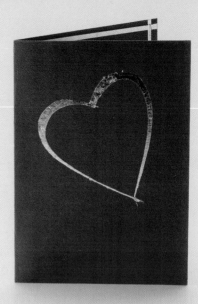

I have a grand passion for pop-up cards. Ever since my first pop-up book at the age of 7, pop-ups have held me enthralled. It's no wonder that I am fascinated with pop-up cards. Big or little … simple or involved, they still fascinate me. They are always a surprise!

Materials

Red card stock or 2
    ready-made red cards
Sheet of gold leaf
Gold-leaf pen
Scissors
Small brush or pompom
3-inch-square piece of
    red-liner industrial-
    strength double-sided
    tape sheet
Glue

1 Make or purchase two red 4¼ x 5½-inch side-fold cards.

2 Close one card, and cutting through both layers, cut ½ inch off the top and ¼ inch off the side opposite the fold. This will be the inner card. *Note: You will have a ¼-inch margin on all four sides when both cards are glued together.*

I've used the very-easy-to-draw heart as the illustration, but any subject that matches on both sides can be used. Draw a snowman, a gingerbread-type doll, a Christmas tree, a pumpkin, a flower, etc. Any symmetrical image will do.

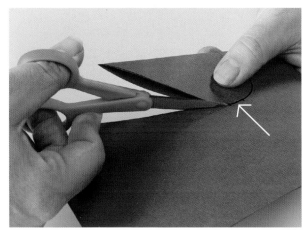

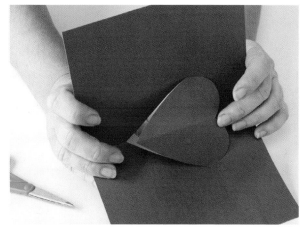

3 With this card still folded, draw half of a heart along the folded edge then cut it out leaving a ½-inch section uncut at the widest part of the curved edge (see arrow). This uncut section will be the only thing still connecting the heart to the card.

4 Open the card and push the cut-out heart forward, refolding the center crease in the heart so it is now a mountain fold. The card itself has a valley fold down the center.

5 Fold a square of red-liner double-stick tape in half with the white liner side facing out.

6 Fold the card in half and place the folded tape under the cut-out area with the fold facing out. Trace the half-heart shape.

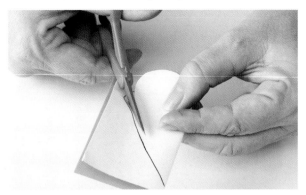

7 Remove the tape from inside of the card, and with the tape still folded, cut out the heart about ⅛ inch inside of the drawn line.

8 Flatten the tape heart and peel off the white backing. This piece should be ⅛ inch smaller than the red heart.

9 Open card, flatten heart and press adhesive-backed heart to it. Peel off red plastic to expose the tape.

10 Cover the heart with the sheet of gold leaf.

11 Smooth gold leaf onto the card and brush away any excess. Save leftover pieces.

12 With the leftover tape piece folded, and referring to the photo, cut out the heart on the drawn line. Peel off the backing. You should have a ⅛-inch outline of a heart. Adhere to the front of the outer card, remove liner and apply gold leaf (see photo on page 24). Attach the two cards to make one with a ¼-inch margin on all four sides of the inner card. Use a gold-leaf pen to write your sentiments and highlight the inside card edges. ■

Stamped Pop-up Card

Masking adds another dimension to this stamped pop-up card.

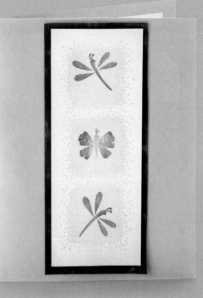

Materials

2 purchased or
   handmade cards
Card stock
Rubber stamps: daisy,
   dragonfly, butterfly,
   Shadow Stamp Trio
Ink pads: black, yellow
Colored pencils
Ribbon
Markers
Craft knife
Cutting mat
Scissors
Glue

1 Make or purchase two standard 4¼ x 5½-inch cards of the same or different colors.

2 Fold one card in half, and cutting through both layers, cut ½ inch off the top and ¼ inch off the side opposite the fold. This will be the inner card. *Note: You will have a ¼-inch margin on all four sides when the cards are glued together.*

3 Stamp a daisy on the inside of the inner card, making certain that the center crease in the card is positioned exactly down the center of the stamped image.

4 Open the card and cut out the image using a craft knife, leaving the matching connecting sections (hinges) on each side of the image. ***Note:*** *You may have to experiment from time to time as to the best place to leave the connecting hinges. If you leave them too high, the image will angle too far up when the card is opened. If you leave them too low the image will face down. Most often the center of the side of the image is the preferred position. Reverse the crease down the center of the cutout making it a mountain fold.*

5 Flatten the daisy again and mask it while you stamp surrounding daisies.

6 Color as desired. Ours are colored using pencils.

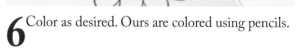

7 The dimensional stems are made by folding several pieces of green card stock in half.

8 Cut the length along the crease. *Note: Credit for the clever dimensional stems goes to Michael Strong of Michael Strong Rubber Stamps. He demonstrated it on the show one day.*

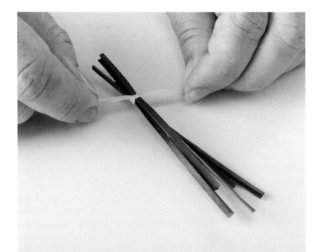

9 Gather several stems and tie together with a ribbon. Attach to card by slipping the top of the stems under the pop-up flower and gluing under the bow. The ends of the stems are free.

10 Attach the two cards to make one with a ¼-inch margin on all four sides. Decorate the front of the card with card-stock panels stamped with dragonflies and a butterfly. The sentiment for the inside of the card was generated on a computer. The Shadow Stamp Trio is inked with a yellow ink pad, and the dragonfly and butterfly images were inked with markers. ■

Illustrated Pop-up Cards

This card is the easiest and most versatile pop-up to make because any image that will fit inside the card can be used. If you have ever made pop-ups, I'm guessing that this is the one you started with—two cuts are all you need.

Materials

Card stock or ready-made cards

Cutouts or stamped images

Scissors

Glue

1 Make or purchase two standard 4¼ x 5½-inch cards of the same or different colors.

2 Fold one card in half and cut ½ inch off the top and ¼ inch off the side opposite the fold. This will be the inner card. You will have a ¼-inch margin on all four sides when the cards are glued together.

3 With the inner card folded, cut two matching slashes cutting from the folded edge toward the open edge (Fig. 1). The cuts should be about ½ inch apart.

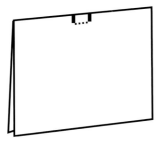

Fig. 1
Cut on heavy lines.
Fold on dashed line.

4 With the card still folded, fold the section between the two cuts upward. Turn card over and repeat the process. Open the card and push this section up into a mountain fold (Fig. 2).

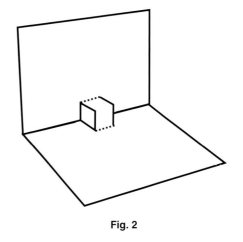

Fig. 2

5 Glue your selected image to the protruding tab. This can be placed so the card is opened vertically or horizontally.

6 Attach the two cards to make one with a ¼-inch margin on all four sides of the inner card.

7 Continue decorating the inside and the front of the card as desired. Our Thank You card was decorated with rubber-stamped images; some were given dimension by attaching them to the card with adhesive-backed foam squares. Our Congratulations card was decorated with stamped words plus a real surprise inside. They're perfect for the occasion. ■

Two-for-One Cards

Two for one? Look closely and you will see that each card is not only a greeting card, but it also contains a pull-off refrigerator magnet. I got so carried away with the idea that I put two magnets on one card!

Materials

School Picture Card
Card stock: white, red
Photograph
Peel-off magnetic strips
Frame rubber stamp
Dye-based ink pad
Colored markers
Tape
Craft knife

Birthday Card
Card stock: white, light
   brown, coral
Photograph and/or
   quotation
Peel-off magnetic strips
Frame rubber stamp
Embossing powder
Heat embossing tool
Craft knife
Tape
Pigment ink pad
Colored markers
Computer with printer

Project note: The two-for-one feature calls for adding a framed quotation or photograph, and attaching matching peel-off magnetic strips to the back of the framed item and to the top surface of the card. The detachable photo or quotation can be placed on either the front or the inside of the card. In the case of our birthday card, there is one on both the front and the inside!

School Picture to Grandma

1 Score and fold an 8½ x 5½-inch piece of red card stock in half crosswise to create a 4¼ x 5½-inch card.

2 On white card stock, stamp, color and cut out frame and center opening. Tape photo to the back side of the frame and add a short length of peel-off magnetic strip to the back of the photo.

3 Cut a matching length of magnetic strip and place it either on the front of the card or on the back side of the front panel to match the position on the photo.

4 Have the youngster write his/her salutation on white card stock; cut out and attach as shown. A note to Grandma can be written on the inside of the card.

Birthday Card

1 Score and fold an 8½ x 5½-inch piece of white card stock in half crosswise to create a 4¼ x 5½-inch card. On the white card stock, stamp, emboss, color and cut out a frame, leaving a narrow border around the stamped image. Cut out center opening as well. Tape a photo to the back of the frame and add a short magnetic strip on the back of the photo.

2 Cut a 2¼ x 2½-inch piece of light brown card stock and layer it on a 2½ x 2¾-inch piece of coral card stock. Attach a short magnetic strip to the top piece of card stock.

3 Print out the words "Another Birthday? Not To Worry …" on white card stock; cut out and adhere to the brown card stock; cut out leaving a small border and attach to the front of the card.

4 Attach narrow strips of the coral card stock to the front of the card along the side edges.

5 Adhere a 3¾ x 5-inch piece of coral card stock to the inside of the card, and attach a magnetic strip the top of it.

6 Print the quotation on white card stock and attach to a piece of the light brown card stock cut slightly larger. Add magnetic strip to back. ■

Hearts Galore Cards

From one basic idea many projects grow … or at least, many variations on a theme. My friend Linda Watson started it all by punching out paper hearts, gluing them to pieces of handmade paper and making color copies. She attached the copies to note cards and stationery, and though the hearts were all copies, no two cards were exactly alike. Some she cut with decorative-edge scissors to resemble stamps. Now I'm guessing that you'll take our suggestions a little further and end up with note cards, stationery, stamps, and who knows what else, that are all your own. You might also try something besides hearts—like cats.

Materials

Variety of handmade papers, preferably highly textured

Plain note cards

Plain stationery

Decorative Japanese paper (optional)

Heart punch

Decorative-edge scissors (optional)

Scanner or copy machine

Adhesive of choice

1 Select a variety of interesting papers either plain or patterned.

2 Cut some of the papers into squares. The squares can be any size; mine are 2½ inches because of the size of the heart punch I used. Punch out a variety of hearts.

3 Try different combinations of hearts and paper squares; when you have selected those you prefer, glue a heart to the center of each square. Line them up and scan them.

4 Print out a number of the scanned hearts, being certain to check the kind of paper you are using. Different settings can give you different results. Try reducing some. Those pictured were reduced 50 percent. Also, change the color setting when scanning. All of the hearts pictured here are the same as those shown in Step 3.

5 Print out the different arrangements, cut them out and attach them to cards or stationery. They can all be the same or different. Or scan an arrangement into your computer and print to create any number of cards or stationery. Cut some individual heart squares with decorative-edged scissors and use as coordinating touches on your envelopes. ∎

Coordinated Envelopes

And of course, don't forget the envelopes. Linda scoured wallpaper sample books and made her envelopes from coordinated wallpaper. This is where printing and adhering a matching heart square to the envelope really makes a difference. The basic envelope pattern is on page 170.

Illuminated Letters

The monks who spent so many hours drawing illuminated images hundreds of years ago probably wouldn't have used the word "fun" to describe how they felt about doing them, but these days we don't have to concern ourselves with making them for posterity, nor do we have to start from scratch. In fact, with all the alphabet rubber stamps in our craft stores, the biggest problem we have is deciding which ones we prefer, and what types of projects to use them on. We've decided they really are fun to make.

Materials

Font of your choice
  (computer, clip art,
  rubber stamp or
  stencil)
80-lb sketch paper,
  watercolor paper or
  equivalent
Black fine-point
  permanent ink pen
Colored pencils or pens
Gold metallic marker or
  gold-leaf pen
Paper adhesive
Adhesive foam dots

For gold leafing
Gold-leaf adhesive
Gold leaf or gold foil

For embossing
Gold embossing ink
Gold embossing powder
Solid rubber stamp
Embossing heat tool
Embossing or erasable
  pen

Project note: I find that rubber stamping is the easiest method to use to get started making illuminated letters.

1 Using a solid letter stamp and gold embossing ink, stamp the impression on the selected paper. Emboss with gold embossing powder and embossing heat tool. Draw a border around the image using either an erasable or an embossing pen. Emboss. Draw a second embossed line outside the first. Emboss.

2 Rubber-stamp small images or draw in designs around the letter with a black fine-point permanent ink pen or colored markers. Flowers are often used, but any small and frequently repeated pattern will work. ■

Note: *The distance between the two borders and the distance from the letter depends on the size of the letter and on your own personal taste. You may prefer no border at all.*

Other Basic Examples

The letter C was hand-drawn with a gold metallic marker on 80-lb artist sketch paper. The left side of the letter was filled in with colored pencils, and the designs made using a stencil and a gold marker. The paper was torn around the edges, which were then outlined using the gold marker. The entire piece was mounted on an olive-green card using raised adhesive foam dots.

This hand-drawn R was done on 80-lb sketch paper using a gold metallic marker. The same marker was used to draw a border around the piece which was then used to decorate this handmade writer's journal.

The letter C was printed out in the Old English Text MT 72-point size using the computer. Gold leaf adhesive was applied with a toothpick, and when tacky, gold foil (not gold leaf) was applied. This is the shiniest of all. The same gold metallic marker used for the other letters was used to border this letter, as well as the card to which it is adhered. The flowers were drawn with the black permanent fine-point ink pen and colored with pencil.

The stamped letter B was filled in using gold leaf, as were the scrolls and the outline of the inside designs. All of the adhesive was applied with a toothpick. Blue-colored pencil and black permanent marker were used to color the inside of the letter. The paper on which the letter was stamped was cut out and layered on black and gold paper, which was centered on the black card.

The easiest and most dramatic of all is this red card with the individual letters stamped and embossed using gold embossing ink and gold embossing powder. The letters were stamped on red card stock, cut out leaving a ⅛-inch border, and layered on a single piece of gold metallic card stock, which was cut around the outside edges with decorative scissors. The entire piece was then attached to the card itself with adhesive foam dots.

Note

With the nice variety of basic cards available on the market today, you can choose to buy cards with cutouts in the fronts or buy a packet of plain cards and make your own.

"Leftovers" Cards

Writing about leftovers doesn't sound too appealing, but as a crafter, I'm sure that you have your share. I know that I do. Often when I start on a project there is a certain amount of experimentation involved to see if my idea will really work. By the time I actually make the project, I have a bunch of projects or parts of projects that I can't really use, but that I can't bear to throw away ... leftovers. So I stash them. This time, I decided to put them in cards. By making up a bunch of cards with cut-outs and having envelopes full of left-over bits and pieces, I'm ready to create in a moment. If you have looked through this book, I am certain you have recognized these leftovers.

Materials

Note cards with
  envelopes
Matching or
  coordinating card stock
Ruler
Craft knife
Pencil
Double-stick tape or
  glue stick

Gold metallic marker
  (optional)
Gold fine-point pen
  (optional)
Black fine-point pen
  (optional)

Basic Card

1 On the back side of the front of the card, draw desired cut-out area and cut out using a ruler and craft knife. The size of the cut-out area can vary, as can the exact location. All of the cards measure 4¼ x 5½ inches.

2 After selecting the leftover piece you want to place in the cut-out area, tape it to the back of the front cover, then cover the entire back of the page with a piece of matching card stock cut ⅛ inch smaller than the card front on all four sides.

Tip
To cut a perfectly neat corner, it helps to cut away from the corner instead of into it. Do this from both directions.

An Alternative Method

No matter how easy it sounds to do, cutting a perfect opening can be a bit tricky. Another method is to fold back the edges.

1 Put the point of your craft knife into a corner of your drawn rectangle and make an angle cut to the center. Do this at all four corners so you have cut a large X.

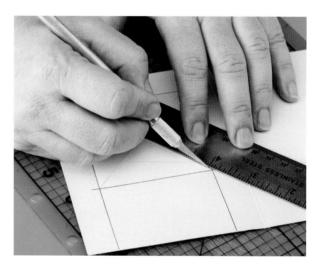

2 Score along each drawn line and fold each cut piece back, making a crisp, sharp fold.

3 Cut off the surplus, cutting to within ½ inch of the fold. Tape or glue the folded paper to hold. Continue as described above. ∎

Our Cards

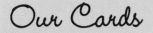

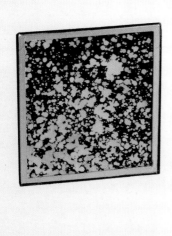

Cut-out area measures 2½ x 2¾ inches. The center is from our Bleach Party project on page 21. Laundry bleach was spritzed on black construction paper. The gold outline wasn't quite as neat around the edges as I wanted, so I outlined the border with a black, fine-point–pen line.

The butterfly is stamped from the same stamp used in the woven cards on page 12, but after embossing it, I colored it with fine-line colored pens. I also added wire antennae. I had no place to use it, so I had put it in the leftover box until this idea came along.

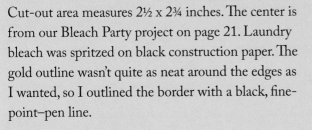

Note: When making something that needs the same measurement over and over, I frequently will cut a strip of cardboard the width of the measurement and use that instead of a ruler. This is what I used on the above two cards when drawing the top and side measurements on one card and on all sides on the other. Instead of measuring ¾ inches at both the top and bottom of each edge, I cut a cardboard strip ¾-inch wide. It saved measuring 13 times.

Here the cutout measures 2½ x 3 inches and is filled with a piece of paper from our chalk-marbleized paper project on page 104.

Scrapbook Paper Cards & Envelopes

I'm quite sure that every scrapbooker out there has long since discovered many uses for all that beautiful paper on and beyond scrapbooking, but what about the few holdouts who have not yet gotten into this popular pastime? I daresay that you are probably aware of the many and varied types of paper in the craft and scrapbooking stores, but possibly you've not stopped long enough to think of the many applications those sheets can be put to besides scrapbooking. Making your own almost-instant note cards is just one possibility.

Materials

- Scrapbook paper (8½ x 11-inch or 12 x 12-inch)
- Craft knife
- Metal-edged ruler
- Pencil
- Small scissors
- Bone folder
- 4½-x5¾-inch piece of cardboard
- Waxed paper
- Cutting mat
- White glue
- Small bowl
- Small paintbrush
- White vinegar

Project notes: You will be able to get two cards from one sheet of paper. If you want matching envelopes, you will need two more sheets. Our cards were all made using 8½ x 11-inch sheets. One cut is all you need take.

The pages are sold individually or in tablet form and come in a variety of weights. If you buy the individual sheets, be sure to check the back of the page that sometimes carries the manufacturer's name—you may want to remove that.

The Cards

1 Using your ruler and craft knife, cut an 8½ x 11-inch sheet of paper in half crossways. Score each resulting piece in half crossways; fold along the scored line and press with a bone folder. You will have two 4¼ x 5½-inch cards.

2 No matter how carefully you score or how neatly you fold, it is easy to discover that the edges don't always line up perfectly. Using the ruler and craft knife, cut through both layers of the folded card, removing about ⅛ inch along the uneven edges.

The Envelopes

1 Cut an 8-inch square of paper that matches or coordinates with your card. With the paper wrong side up, place the waxed-paper–wrapped cardboard diagonally in one corner with the two bottom corners about ½ inch from the side edges of the paper and an equal distance from the bottom point.

2 Fold the left side of the paper in and crease firmly. Repeat with the right side of the paper. The two points should face each other in the center.

3 Fold the bottom point of the paper up. It should overlap the side edges of the two sides and extend slightly beyond the center. Fold the top point down. Press all folds neatly using the bone folder.

4 Unfold all four points. Remove cardboard, flatten paper and cut out the four corners where creased. Round off the outside corners.

5 Return cardboard to the center of the paper sheet and fold in the two side points again. With a small brush, carefully apply white glue along the two lower angled edges. Fold up the bottom point and press into place.

Note

To create a custom-fit envelope for any card, create the cardboard template ¼ inch wider and longer than your card. Wrapping the template in waxed paper will help keep the glue from spreading where it doesn't belong.

6 In a small bowl, mix one tablespoon of white vinegar with two tablespoons of white glue. With the small paintbrush, apply this mixture along the two side edges of the top point of the envelope. Wait a few seconds for it to dry, then apply another coat. When this coat is dry, fold the top over.

7 When you use the envelope, moisten the flap as you would on any commercial envelope. ∎

Tips for Making Envelopes

Whether you buy or make the envelopes, you want your cards and envelopes to look as if they were made for each other. Take your time to make certain they are coordinated in both look and feel. The texture of the papers should be similar and the colors should be compatible. If making your own envelopes:

- Use another sheet of the same scrapbook paper and make a matching envelope.

- Use a sheet of paper that has a color repeated in the card and make a coordinating envelope.

- No matter what colors are in the card, if it has a noticeable amount of white in it, any white envelope can be used.

- Whether matching a white or a colored envelope to your card, the effect of a matching set can be enhanced by lining the envelope with the paper used to make the card.

- If you are making your own envelope, it is easier to add the lining paper before gluing the envelope together.

- If using a commercial envelope, you can easily open it by applying the heat from a heat gun. Open flat and then glue in the lining and refold the envelope. No additional glue will be needed to hold it together.

Paper Napkin Cards

At one time, this was my chosen method for making my own note cards. It's still a wonderful way to make note cards, especially now, with all the special-occasion napkins and decorative tissue papers that are available, as well as rubber stamps, punches and all manner of embellishments. You can easily turn them into greeting cards for any occasion.

Materials

Matte-finish white or
   light-color card
Decorative paper
   napkins or tissue paper
Plastic wrap
Scissors
Iron and ironing board

1 Open napkin. Most decorative napkins will have a border of indented dots. Remove this border with scissors. Peel off the top layer of the napkin. *Note: If using tissue paper, this step is unnecessary.*

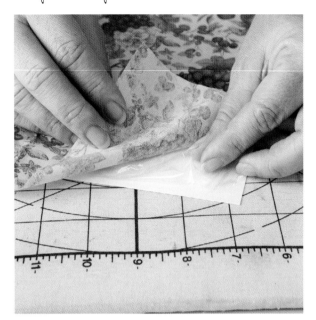

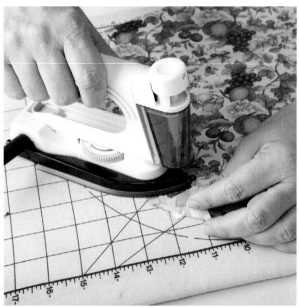

2 Open card and place right side up on ironing surface. Cover with a piece of the plastic wrap cut slightly larger than the card. Smooth it out with your hand. Cover this with the top layer of the napkin. Be certain that no plastic extends beyond the edges of the napkin.

3 Press with a medium iron. Move the iron slowly across the surface of the napkin or tissue, making certain there is no exposed plastic that the iron might touch. You might have to go over some areas more than once to be certain that the three layers— the paper napkin, the plastic wrap and the card—are completely and smoothly laminated.

4 Wait until the card is completely cool before moving it. With scissors, carefully and neatly trim off the napkin and plastic that extend beyond the edge of the card.

5 Gently create a crisp fold with a bone folder. ■

Tip

A June Tailor combination padded ironing mat and cutting mat is ideal for this project, or you can iron on a magazine.

If at any time you see that there is a spot where the paper has separated from the card you can go back and re-iron that spot.

If making your own card rather than using a commercial one, you can apply the napkin before cutting and folding the card.

You might want to line your envelopes to match. If using a commercial envelope, cut a piece of paper to use as a lining, iron the napkin to it, and then fold and insert in the envelope.

And then I tried ...

Gift-wrapping paper, tissue paper, handmade paper and origami paper. The gift-wrapping paper and tissue paper worked fine much of the time, but not always. The handmade paper and origami paper didn't work at all. The napkins are still the best.

The cards on page 48:

• The multicolored purple, gold, green, etc. card is gift-wrapping paper.
• The pale green card with flowers and butterflies is a paper napkin.
• The black and white polka-dot card is tissue paper.

Just Because

I must admit to being just a tad embarrassed about this chapter title. We all know where it came from and what the next line is: "Because I said so." (There was even a movie with that title, and everyone knew why.) The embarrassing part is that it's true. There were a number of projects that I wanted included in the book that really didn't fit into any particular category, but I wanted them in. It was to be my book, so I pulled out the mother line, then softened it a bit by saying these projects would be in "just because" ... "just because I like them." I hope you will try some of them for the same reason, and that you will enjoy making them ... just because.

Pop-up Packages

We have pop-up books and pop-up cards so why not pop-up packages? With so many gift-giving occasions throughout the year, and so many folks who aren't too confident about their bow-making or gift-wrapping ability, pop-up packaging might be just the answer. For those who have packages that must be sent through the mail, and who hate having the bows squashed, this seems to be the perfect solution. The packages are flat until you match up the hook-and-loop pieces, and suddenly, you have a pop-up!

Materials

Gift-wrapped package

Pop-up cutouts from gift wrap, photographs, rubber-stamped images, greeting cards, etc.

Card stock (optional)

Matching gift wrap

80-lb watercolor paper, or heavy-weight construction paper

Hook-and-loop tape

Double-sided low-tack tape

Glue

1 Wrap the package as desired, then select materials to be used for pop-ups. *Note: Our package features rubber stamped images of gift packages, stars cut from the wrapping paper and a photo. When using cutouts from lightweight paper, adhere them to a piece of card stock to give them body.*

2 Cut a piece of watercolor paper the width of the package or a few inches narrower. Cut it the same length or slightly shorter than the length of the package. *Note: On the pictured package, I used heavyweight blue construction paper in lieu of the watercolor paper.*

3 Fold the paper in half crosswise, then make accordion pleats from the fold toward each end of the paper. You should have at least four mountain folds. Each pleat should be about ¾ inch wide so it will be deep enough to support the cutouts.

4 Place the pleated strip on top of the package, making certain that the first fold from the end of the package on both sides is a valley fold so the extending paper on each side lies flat.

5 Place several cutouts temporarily in the valley folds to get an idea of how things are going to look. Remove the cutouts. Cut two pieces of the leftover gift-wrapping paper the same width as the watercolor paper and twice the length of the unpleated section. Glue these strips onto both sides of the construction paper so that only the pleated section is uncovered.

6 Place the various cutouts into the pleats, but hold them in position only temporarily with double-sided, low-tack tape. Holding the front portion secure, lift up the back section and fold it over to the front, matching up the front and back edges. None of the cutout stand-ups should be exposed or stick out on the front or on the sides of the folded piece. Unfold again, and secure the cutouts permanently in place.

7 To attach the pop-up strip to the package, glue or tape the front panel to the front portion of the box top. Close the back panel over the front one and attach two adhesive backed hook-and-loop squares to the two front corners. (See photo on page 54.) Peel off the protective covering, lift the panel and again place it on the back portion of the box top. Press the two corners to firmly attach the hook-and-loop squares to the box top. This is the way the package should look when the recipient opens it.

8 For presentation, unfasten the back corners, bring them up and over the front again and wrap a ribbon around the package to hold everything in position.

9 Add a small gift tag with the recipient's name and instructions to "Remove the ribbon and match up the hook-and-loop squares. Surprise!" ∎

A Christmas pop-up using letters from the gift-wrapping paper. No bow necessary.

Poof Maker

This project is the easiest, fastest and the least-expensive project I have ever made. It's probably also the silliest, but it does the job and that's what counts. If you have occasion to make a bunch of these little pouches of candy or nuts for a birthday party table, a baby or bridal shower, wedding-reception tables, Halloween treats, or any such occasion, this little shoe box with a hole in it will make the job much quicker and easier. Plus it helps in decorating gift packages, too!

Materials

Shoe box or equivalent

Empty bathroom tissue cardboard core

Pen or pencil

9- or 12-inch circles of nylon net or tulle, cellophane, tissue paper or Mylar*

Small candy or nuts

Narrow ribbon

Small sharp scissors or craft knife

Tape or glue (optional)

Most of my candy pouches are made from 12-inch circles. A dinner plate is perfect to use for a pattern.

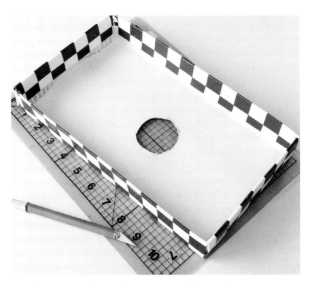

1 Stand cardboard core vertically on the center of the box top. Draw around it and cut out the circle.

2 Center two or three stacked circles over the hole in the box; place the upright cardboard core on top of the circles over the hole.

3 Pour candy or nuts down the tube and then push the tube down into the box. You may need to experiment a few times to see how much candy or nuts to pour in. Remove the tube.

4 Partially lift the box top and reach inside with your other hand to grab hold of the gathered tulle or paper.

5 Pull the candy pouch out from underneath the box top; tie a ribbon around the paper or fabric to hold the pouch together. Separate the tulle or paper layers to make it full and poofy.

Photo 1   **Photo 2**   **Photo 3**

Options

Depending on the occasion and material used for the circles, the number of circles you will use will vary.

For party treats or decorations, two layers of purple and green Mylar paper will no doubt be sufficient; candy-coated chocolates are perfect for the filling (photo 1).

For wedding-reception tables, candy-coated almonds are frequently the choice with two or three tulle circles (photo 2).

For a baby shower, two or three pink or blue nylon net circles or iridescent cellophane circles work well (photo 3).

Green and red circles, either separately or together, are great for Christmas festivities. Anything colorful is good for a birthday party. It's a very personal choice.

To make it all even easier, you can frequently buy Mylar circles in the party department of your local craft store. Tulle circles are often available in the wedding department. ■

But Wait ... There's More!

Instead of candy, cut a cardboard circle about the size of a 50-cent piece and place it over the shoe-box hole on top of the circles. Push the core down into the box and gather the paper tightly. Tie the ribbon close to the cardboard. Tape or glue to a wrapped box. Mylar works well for this with coordinated gift-wrap paper.

Little Boxes

I doubt there's a crafter out there who hasn't made these little boxes at one time or another. For all the years I've been making them, I still occasionally hear from viewers who have just come across this "new idea" they want to share. The method of folding varies from time to time and viewer to viewer, but the technique I discovered most recently turns out to be older than any of us. Mix these directions with a viewer idea for making angled cuts instead of straight ones, and it's the best and now my favorite.

Materials

Paper materials such
   as old greeting cards,
   scrapbook paper,
   origami paper*, etc.
Ruler
Pencil or pen
Scissors
Bone folder

*I think origami paper is easier to use because it's lightweight.

1 Cut two 6-inch squares from paper; cut the square for the bottom of the box ¼ inch smaller on two adjacent sides than the square for the top. Find the center of the larger square by drawing diagonal lines from corner to corner on the wrong side.

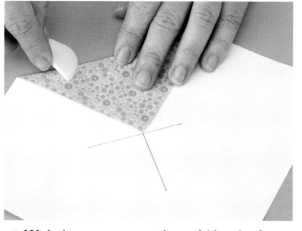

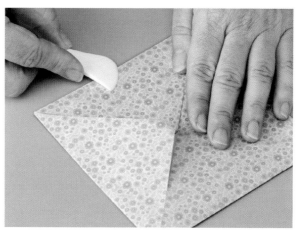

2 With the paper wrong side up, fold each of the corners to the center and crease well along the folds.

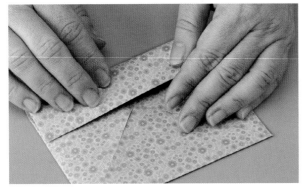

3 Fold one of the side edges in to the center and crease well. Unfold. Repeat this step with the remaining three sides.

4 Open one flap and make an angled cut to the first crease line as indicated in photo. Make a second cut on the other side of the flap. Open the flap on the opposite side and make two identical cuts at that end. **Note:** *The advantage of using this method of cutting at an angle is that none of the raw edges will show.*

5 Fold the two side points on the top flap in toward each other.

6 Bring the sides of the box up and fold the two end tabs in toward each other.

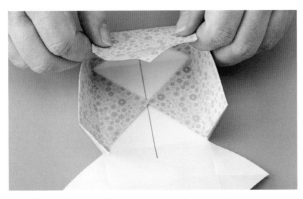

7 Bring the top flap over the tabs and down into the box. Repeat at other end to complete the box.

8 Repeat the entire process with the smaller square to make the box bottom. ∎

Note

If using greeting cards to create the boxes, the front of the card is used as the top of the box and the back of the card is used for the bottom of the box.

Alternative Version

This is where all this folding started many years ago. A true origami piece means no cutting … not even those little angle cuts … but it also means no raw edges either.

1 Follow steps 1–3 of original version.

2 Open one flap as noted in step 4 but do not make any cuts. Instead, fold in the two side edges of the flap as you bring up the side edges of the box, then bring the top flap over and down into the box. Do this at both ends. Our photos shows the second end being folded, so that the box is now complete.

Once you get this method down pat, you can make these boxes practically in a nanosecond, although it is a bit tricky when using heavier card stock.

Note

So what's the big deal about having no raw edges show? Unless you are a hard-core purist about such things, this probably makes no difference to you. However, if you are making fabric-covered versions, not having raw and/or fraying edges makes a big difference as evidenced in this box sent in by Betty Venable of Tehachapi, Calif. Look ma … no raw edges!

Sharon's Boxes

Sharon Kennedy, of Foster, Calif., sent in a grand selection of boxes. Some were decorated with beads, charms and decoupage. One box was embossed with embossing powder and a few were personalized with my name. For the most elegant box tops, she glued beautiful silk fabric to card stock before folding. In most cases, the bottoms of the boxes were made from black card stock.

But we're not done yet ...

For those who wonder what to do with these little boxes once you've made them, Sharon filled a number of hers with gifts ranging from miniature handmade books to jewelry. One contained a piece of chocolate wrapped in gold foil nestled in metallic gold tissue paper! Even that single piece of chocolate seemed elegant. Remember, presentation is everything!

Speaking of presentation ... read on. There's more!

Several years ago, I received a sweet letter from Donna Pence telling about her 82-year-old father, Richard Smith of Titusville, Fla. Donna wrote that her father "has been making these tiny boxes out of used greeting cards for about eight years. He likes to give them to people, especially waitresses at local restaurants. He puts their tip inside and writes a special note for them on the bottom."

If you've never made these little boxes, try them. Once you start you may think of a number of reasons for making more. If you've made them in the past, try them again. You may surprise yourself at the uses you'll think of!

Paper Flower Napkin Rings

I wish I had a quarter for every one of these napkin rings I've made. I would have been independently wealthy by now. Although I've always made these from felt, for this book I decided to try tissue paper ... and it worked! I'm guessing that everything could as easily be made from crepe paper, mulberry paper or handmade paper. I just didn't happen to have any of those papers on hand when the idea struck.

Materials

Tissue papers: red, green

Tracing paper

Pencil

Scissors

Paintbrush (optional)

Acrylic medium
  (optional)

1 Trace each of the pattern pieces onto tracing paper and cut out. Use the patterns on page 171 to trace and cut inner and outer flower petals from red tissue paper and leaves from green tissue paper. Fold outer flower petals and leaf piece on fold lines, and with scissors, cut slits in the folded pieces as indicated on pattern. Unfold.

shown in the main photo. Gently slide a rolled-up napkin into the loop below the flower. ∎

2 Bring the end petals of the inner flower petals piece together. Fold, but do not crease, the center section in thirds lenthwise and carefully push it through the slits in the outer flower petals and the leaf piece. From the other side pull this center section through until the bottom of the center petals touch the outer petals. Carefully shape petals as

Tip

If desired, before assembling, brush acrylic medium onto leaves and let dry for a bit of added strength.

One-Sheet Mini Books

These are in the group of what I refer to as "good things to know" because you just never know when you might want to make one of these little fold-and-cut books. Made from a single sheet of paper, these can become note cards, greeting cards, scrapbook inserts, or carry-along photo books. They can be used for writing letters, journaling your thoughts or for impressing your friends with your cleverness. The basic folds have been around for awhile, but just in case you forgot or just never knew how, here are the fold-and-cut directions. You supply the decorative finishing touches.

Materials

8½ x 11-inch sheets of paper, desired colors	Ribbon
	Ruler
Cardboard or card stock	Scissors or craft knife
Various printed papers	Glue stick
Photographs, stickers, punch-outs, rubber stamps, etc.	

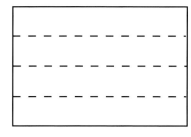

Fig. 1

Book #1

1 Place an 8½ x 11-inch sheet of paper horizontally on work surface and fold it in half lengthwise. Unfold. Fold each end into the center fold line; unfold (Fig. 1).

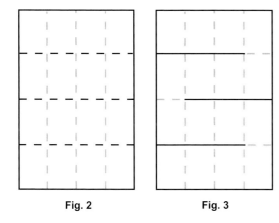

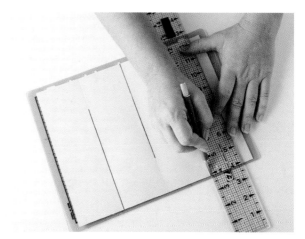

2 Turn the paper a quarter turn so it is now vertical and repeat the folds. You should now have 16 small rectangles on paper as indicated by dashed lines on Fig. 2.

Fig. 2　　Fig. 3

3 Make three horizontal cuts as indicated by solid lines on Fig. 3.

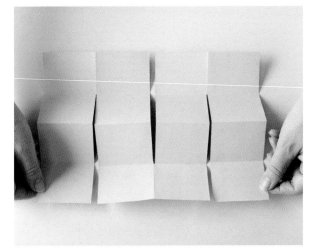

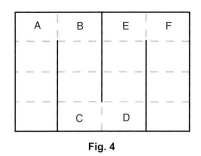

Fig. 4

4 Starting at the lower left corner, fold the first rectangle up toward you; fold back on the next fold, up on the next and continue in the same manner until the entire sheet of paper is folded and you have a small accordion-folded book.

Note: *To make folding easier, refer to Fig. 4 and adhere the reverse sides of "A" and "B" rectangles together; repeat with "C" and "D" rectangles and "E" and "F" rectangles. This will form one long strip which can then be accordion-folded to form a small book.*

5 Cut two squares of cardboard or card stock slightly larger than one of the book pages. Glue each square to a piece of decorative paper cut slightly larger than the square. Fold excess paper to the back and glue to hold. Glue squares to the front and back of the book as covers. Insert a ribbon between the last book page and the back cover, leaving 6-inch ribbon ends extending on each side as a closure.

6 Decorate the blank pages with photographs, stickers, punch-outs, etc., or use the book as a mini journal to write special notes. Close the book and tie shut with ribbon.

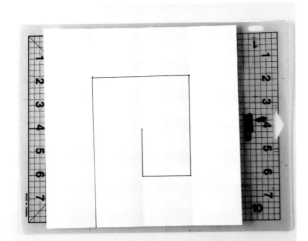

Book #2

1 Cut a square sheet of paper; ours measured 8½ inches square. Fold paper in the same manner as for Book #1, forming 16 small squares instead of rectangles.

Note: *This book is read by opening it and returning it to its original flattened state, so any decorating, rubber-stamping, writing, etc. is best done at this point, when you can see where it will go on the finished page.*

2 Starting one square in from the lower left side of the page, cut from the bottom edge up to the bottom edge of the top square; turn and cut along the fold to the edge of the last square. Referring to photo, continue cutting in a spiral fashion until the center of the page is reached (Fig. 5).

3 Beginning in lower left corner, accordion-fold paper until you once again have a small book.

4 Cut two squares of cardboard or card stock the same size as the book pages; adhere printed paper to each square, wrapping the excess paper to the back. Glue to the first and last pages of the book. Secure with a ribbon. This time the book is decorated to be given to someone else as a birthday card surprise! ■

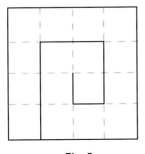

Fig. 5

Dodecahedron Mobile

This project is one of my all-time favorites. I first saw one of these mobiles hanging in crafter/designer/inventor Patricia Nimocks' kitchen and fell in love with it. It took me a while to figure it out, but when I did, I hung it in my office until it turned yellow. Even then I thought I could rejuvenate it with paint, but instead I dropped it and accidentally stepped on it. It was time to make another one. The original version consisted of two watercolor-paper dodecahedrons (a polyhedron with 12 faces), one inside the other. As you can see from the pictures, that was only the beginning. I have been making variations of it on and off ever since.

Materials

90-lb watercolor paper or card stock

Small sharp scissors (cuticle scissors recommended)

Compass

Protractor (optional)

Ruler

Bone folder

Pencil with a very sharp point

Nylon monofilament thread or fishing line

White glue or glue stick

Small brush or toothpick

Small piece of masking tape

Pushpin

Clean hands!

Note

The white double dodecahedron on the left is my latest version of the original. Again, patience and accuracy are very important for this project. Keep your pencil points sharp to keep an extra $1/16$ inch from creeping in every now and then.

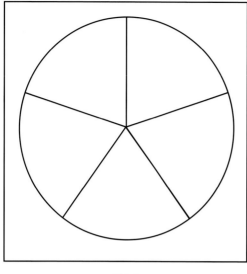

Fig. 1

Fig. 2

Pattern

1 The required pattern is pictured on page 172. Trace it or copy it on a copy machine. Make a hole in the exact center with a pushpin. Remove pin. If you prefer to make your own pattern, use a compass to draw a circle 6 inches or larger, then use a protractor to divide the circle into five equal sections of 72 degrees each. Mark these places with small dots on the circumference of the circle. Using a ruler and a sharp pencil, draw a line from the center of the circle to each one of the dots (Fig. 1).

2 To check the accuracy of your measuring, draw a line between each of the adjacent dots on the circumference. The length of the lines should all be the same (Fig. 2).

Note: On the back of the pattern, place a piece of masking tape over the hole in the center. This hole will be used over and over again, and the tape is to help it resist tearing or stretching.

3 On the watercolor paper, use a compass to draw 12 (4½-inch) circles. Inside each circle, draw a 3-inch circle. Cut out the 4½-inch circles. Do *not* cut out the inside circle. Place one of the circles on top of your pattern, lining up the center holes exactly. Hold everything together with a pushpin. Mark tiny dots along the outside edge of your circle at each of the places where the lines from the center of the pattern circle extend (Fig. 3).

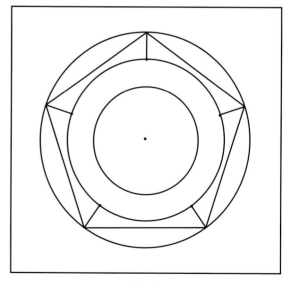

Fig. 3

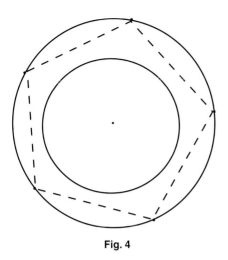

Fig. 4

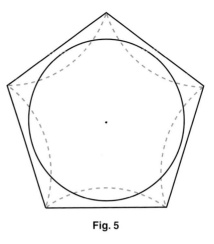

Fig. 5

4 Remove the pattern from the circle and place a ruler between two adjacent dots on the edge of the 4½-inch circle. Use a bone folder or the point of your compass to score a line between the dots. Repeat between each of the adjacent dots around the circle. The end of each scored line should touch but not overlap (Fig. 4).

5 Fold back along each of the scored lines. Run your fingernail or a bone folder along each folded edge to make certain you have a crisp sharp fold. Measure the length of each folded edge. They should all match (Fig. 5). Unfold the flaps.

6 Cut out the center circles. Repeat with each of the remaining 11 circles.

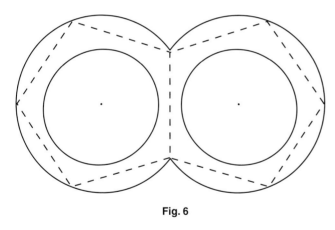

Fig. 6

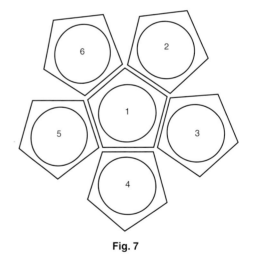

Fig. 7

Assembly

1 Place two circles side by side with the touching flaps folded down. The folds should line up perfectly. Apply white glue to one of the flaps, spreading it with a toothpick or small brush to cover the entire surface. Press the two flaps together (Fig. 6).

2 The sequence in gluing the circles together is a matter of choice. I found it easiest to select one to be the center circle and glue five more around it, attaching one to each of the five sides (Fig. 7). When all six are glued together, you will have a basket-shaped piece. All the flaps should be facing out in the finished piece.

3 Glue the remaining six circles together as you did the first, but do not yet join them to the first six.

4 To make the smaller inner dodecahedron, cut 12 (2-inch) circles with a 1-inch circle cut out of the center. Mark, score, fold and assemble as you did the larger circles.

5 Glue the two halves of the inner dodecahedron together, but before gluing the last circle in

Tip

Hold the circles together with paper clips before gluing them to get an idea of how they should look. Three things to remember: clean hands, sharp scissors, accuracy.

place, tie a good-size knot in a long length of the hanging thread (monofilament thread or fishing line) and place it inside the sphere. Place the thread so it comes up through one of the corners where three circles are joined.

6 Glue the two halves of the outer dodecahedron together around the inner one, but before gluing the last circle in place, pull the hanging thread up through one of the corners where three circles are joined. Be certain to hold the outer dodecahedron up to check that the inner dodecahedron is hanging in the exact center before making the final closure. ■

Note: As warned at the beginning, all folded edges should match perfectly, but chances are at least a few will be slightly off. It's bound to happen. Just match as many as you can. If, however, there is more than 1/16 inch difference on several sides, you may have to make another circle.

But Wait ... There's More!

If mobiles aren't your thing, or even if they are, just turn the flaps to those 12 sides inside and you have a photo frame that can sit on the table or dresser or desk and hold 11 photos, or 10 photos plus one circle with information of who, what, where and when those pictures were taken. If you fill all 12 cutouts with photos, you will have to rotate the frame occasionally so the same person won't be facedown all the time.

The basic directions for making the Multi-Picture Picture Frame are exactly the same for cutting and folding and gluing together, but be certain that when you glue, you have the flaps facing in rather than out. Before the final assembly, glue or tape the

photographs in place, making certain that nobody ends up upside down. Getting the last flap glued will be tricky, but console yourself with the thought that it will be on the bottom and on the inside. Or, leave the space for the 12th circle empty.

Variations

The blue-and-white mobile on page 74 was made with the baby's room in mind. Three single dodecahedrons were cut from coordinated sheets of card stock.

Another mobile for the youngster's room is cut from brightly colored sheets of card stock. Each circle hangs from a monofilament line which was threaded through a 12-inch foam-board circle. The lines are gathered together about 12 inches above the circle, knotted and hung from a large cup hook. The foam board itself was covered, both top and bottom, with pie-shaped pieces of the same-colored card-stock sheets, and the edge of the circle is painted bright green.

The size of the circles and their cut-out centers is arbitrary. The larger the cut-out center circles, the airier looking the mobile.

Fold-up Gift Boxes

There were some decisions that had to be made concerning this project. Did these pretty paper fold-ups really qualify as boxes? It was when we ran down the list of what they could be used for—gift certificates, money and jewelry were immediately mentioned—that it became obvious that if what they would be holding were gifts, then they would most certainly qualify as gift boxes, and practical ones at that. These are boxes that the recipient can fold flat, store in a small space and have ready to use for her own gift-giving when the time arrives.

Materials

150-lb watercolor paper or other
  heavy-weight paper
Tracing paper
Rubber stamps
Ink pads
Colored pencils, pens or watercolors
Ribbon
Bone folder
Scissors
Craft knife (optional)

1 Enlarge and trace provided pattern on page 173 on tracing paper or draw your own to desired size by changing the measurements. Cut out box from watercolor paper or paper of choice. Score on dashed lines as indicated on pattern. Cut the slits for the ribbon with a craft knife, if desired.

2 Decorate as desired using any of the suggested materials such as colored pencils, pens, watercolors, rubber stamps, etc.

3 Fold along all scored lines and press with a bone folder. Unfold.

4 Insert ribbon of choice; run it through two slits, all four slits or none at all. These are only there to make the ribbon seem more a part of the box. It's now ready for gift-giving!

Notes: An alternative method for decorating is to adhere scrapbook paper, gift-wrap or adhesive-backed fabric to the watercolor paper. In this case, it is better to do this before cutting out the pattern.

One of our boxes features scrapbook paper with a travel theme. How perfect for cruise tickets! Another box is covered with adhesive-backed fabric. A slip-off band is used instead of a bow. No slits needed. ■

Tip

For an added personalized touch, rubber-stamp a matching gift tag.

Pretty Pillow Boxes

When I saw my first pillow box, I had no idea it had such a name. I only knew that it was the container that held the shower cap in my hotel room, and I was fascinated with the shape. So I took it home and figured out how to make one, following my own directions. That was many moons ago! These days, not only are pillow boxes everywhere, but you can also find patterns for making them in any number of publications. However, this time we're giving you step-by-step instructions for creating your own pattern to make pillow boxes in any size and in a variety of shapes. That way you can use them to hold a lot more than a shower cap!

Materials

8½ x 11-inch sheet of card stock	Bone folder
	Metal-edge ruler
Piece of paper at least 3½ inches in width	Scissors
	Glue or heavy-duty double-sided tape
Pen or pencil	

Project note: The following directions are for making a 3½ x 5-inch box. When making boxes in other sizes, remember that the horizontal measurement of the card stock must be twice the desired width of the box plus ½ inch for overlap. The vertical measurement should be the desired length of the completed box plus at least a 1-inch allowance at both the top and bottom for the depth of the opening. The larger the box, the deeper that measurement can be. When measuring the pattern for the curved top, the folded piece of paper from which you cut the pattern must be (before folding) the same width as the box, and the placement of the dot from which you start the curved line should be half the depth of the top of the box from the top of the folded piece.

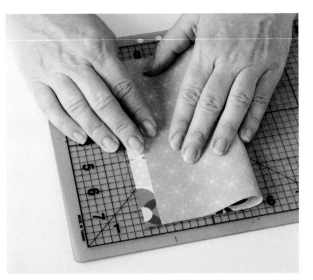

1 From a standard 8½ x 11-inch sheet of card stock, cut a piece that measures 7 x 7½ inches. Place the piece wrong side up with the 7½-inch side horizontal on work surface. *Note: This is double-sided paper. The flower print will be the inside of the box.*

2 Fold card stock almost in half vertically, leaving a ½-inch extension along one side edge.

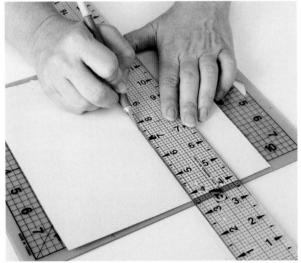

3 Score and fold the ½-inch extension over the edge of the other half of the sheet; press along each fold with a bone folder. This piece will be the box. Set aside.

4 Cut a piece of paper the same width as the width of the box. In this case, it will be 3½ inches. The length is incidental.

5 Fold paper in half horizontally bringing the 3½ inch ends together, then fold the folded piece in half vertically.

6 With the folded edges at the left and the double folded edges at the bottom, mark a dot on the folded side edge ½ inch up from the bottom. Draw a gentle curve from this dot to the opposite right lower corner of the folded bottom edge.

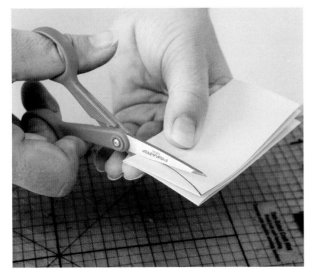

7 Cut out along the curve, cutting through all the layers. Unfold.

8 Place this cutout along the top edge of the folded box from step 3 and trace around the top (outside) edge.

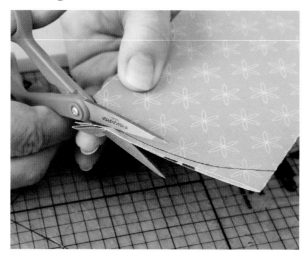

9 Remove pattern and cut out along this line, cutting through both layers of the box. Repeat along the bottom edge of the box.

10 Replace the cutout along the top edge of the box and trace along the bottom (inside) curved line. Repeat at the opposite end of the box. Turn the box over and repeat on the other side. Score along all four drawn lines.

11 Unfold box piece and press along all the curved scored lines, folding the scored lines in toward what will be the inside of the box. This may be a bit tricky at first. Take your time and do it carefully.

12 With a pair of small scissors, cut out a small half circle along the outside edge of one of the curved edges at what will be the box top and another along the outside edge of the curved edge at the other end of the box.

13 Apply glue or double-sided tape along the overlapping tab along the edge of the box. Fold box, placing this extending tab on the inside, and press together tightly.

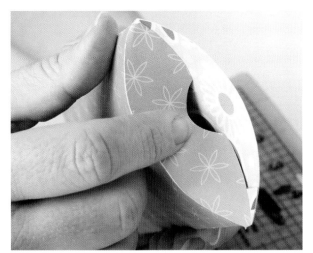

Tip

A bonus is the fact that these can be folded flat. Make up a bunch and stack them away in no space at all to have on hand for the next time you need a small gift box.

14 Press the top flap with the half-circle cutout in toward the inside of the box, followed by the other flap. Repeat at the bottom. Be certain to place the flap with the half circle cutout in place first. Box completed! Whew! ■

More Ideas

After I first demonstrated making these pillow boxes on my show, I received some delightful responses from viewers. One viewer wrote that she used Christmas cards to make a number of boxes that she then filled with red-and-white Christmas candies. *Note: I immediately tried this. Using cards is a great idea! Use the entire card; put "To:" and "From:" stickers on the back and use it as a way to "wrap" small Christmas gifts.*

DuAnne Sonneville of Orchard Lake, Mich., wrote that she used the idea for table favors at her daughter Kirsten's college graduation dinner. DuAnne first photocopied a number of photographs from important times in her daughter's life (prom, high school graduation, school plays, band, etc.), then cut out the faces and made a collage onto the shape of the pillow box she would be making. She returned to the copy shop and had the collage photocopied onto the sheets of card stock from which she made the boxes and then filled them with Kirsten's favorite candy, peanut M&Ms. She said they made for a great conversation piece as well as nice mementos.

Shortly after seeing this idea on the show, Crystal Varnadore of Boynton Beach, Fla., wrote that she liked DuAnne's suggestion so much she made pillow-box favors for her best friend's bridal shower. She covered them with photographs of her best friend and then filled them with Dove chocolates. She, too, said they were a big hit.

I have a feeling these ideas are only the beginning. What an easy way to make something very personal for any special occasion.

Mizuhiki Decorated Gift Boxes

Karen Thomas made a card on my show with a Mizuhiki cord Christmas tree on it. I loved it and thought that the technique could certainly be used to make other things. A decorated box is what I came up with. There's no need to wrap your gift if you give it in something like this. In fact, the box itself can be the gift, and afterwards, it can sit on a table as a decoration. Cherryl designed our bubble-covered box made in dramatic shades of blue and green.

Materials

- Mizuhiki cords: light blue, dark blue, green
- Gessoed papier-mâché box
- Lumiere pearl turquoise acrylic paint
- Paintbrush
- Bone folder (optional)
- Red-liner industrial-strength double-sided adhesive sheet*
- Personal die-cut machine
- Circle die with 4 circles** or craft knife and ruler
- Scissors
- Glue

*The industrial-strength double-sided adhesive comes in sheets as well as spools of tape and is available in most craft stores or rubber-stamp stores. It goes by a number of different names. We refer to it as red-liner tape for easy identification.

**If you do not have access to a die-cut machine, a craft knife and ruler can be used. However, straight-sided shapes are preferred to circles in this case.

1 Paint papier-mâché box and top with pearl turquoise paint. Set aside to dry.

2 Cut the sheet of double-sided adhesive into four, approximately 4 x 5-inch, pieces. **Note:** *You may have a bit left over; save it for another use.*

Note

No need to worry about damage to the table. These cords may look like metal and act like metal, but they are solid paper—twisted paper—and are totally safe.

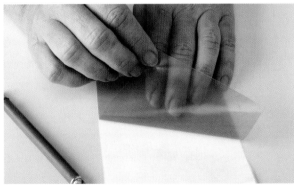

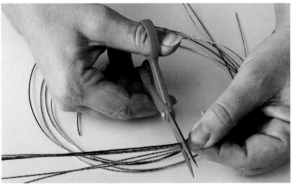

3 Peel off one side of one of the adhesive pieces and place on work surface sticky side up. Cut a number of the cords slightly longer than the adhesive piece is wide and start lining up the cords on the tape.

4 You can work from one end to the other, or start in the middle and work out. Our cords were selected randomly concerning color. The important thing is that each cord be lined up perfectly next to the previous one. Push them together with a bone folder or your fingernail until the sheet is full.

5 When the adhesive is completely covered, trim extending edges and put the sheet on the die and into the die cut machine, following manufacturer's directions.

6 Cut out four circles in graduated sizes. Or use a ruler and sharp craft knife and cut any number of straight-sided shapes. In either case, repeat the process of covering the tape with the Mizuhiki cords and cutting the shapes until you have enough cutouts to satisfactorily cover the box. We used 9½ circles.

7 Peel off the adhesive backing on the cut-out circles.

8 Place circles randomly on the box lid and around the sides of the box. Use semicircles on the edges. Press to hold.

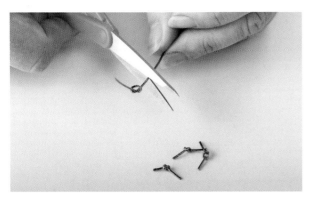

9 Tie six knots in a length of green paper cord. Cut each knot off of the cord as you make it.

10 Attach each knot with a dot of glue on each side of the box lid.

11 Run a bead of clear glue along the bottom edge of the box and attach a length of paper cord. Repeat along the top edge of the lid for a finished look. ∎

Rectangular Box

This box was decorated in basically the same way, except that two-color (red/gold) Mizuhiki cords were used, along with plain red and plain gold cords. They were placed in a planned pattern of three red, three gold and three red/gold on the box top, and solid red on the insert. First, a 3 x 4-inch piece of tape was covered in solid red cords. Next, a piece of the tape was cut to exactly fit the top of the box. This was covered with red, gold and red/gold cords. When both pieces of tape were completely covered, a diamond shape was cut from the center of each piece. The box-top piece was peeled and placed in

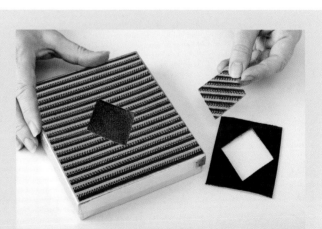

position, and the red diamond peeled and inserted in the center. The remaining diamond and the red cutout are waiting for another home.

Match the Cutouts

This project is a great learning tool for the little ones to enjoy. I made mine using gift-wrap paper, but if you're a rubber stamper, you might find it more crafting fun to stamp your own paper.

Materials

Gift-wrap paper with
  simple easy-to-cut-out
  figures*
Poster board or stiff
  card stock
Metal cookie sheet or
  countertop protector
Clear Contact paper or
  several laminating
  sheets

Magnetic strips
Scissors
Tape
Glue stick

*Make your own paper by rubber-stamping a sheet of white
paper, available in rolls at office-supply stores. Butcher wrap or
freezer wrap can also be used.*

1 Select gift-wrap paper that has easy-to-cut figures or designs such as balloons, animals, circles, etc. If figures are too detailed, cut around them, leaving a ½-inch border.

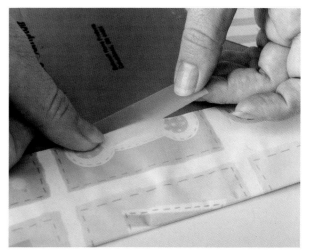

2 Cover the cookie sheet or countertop protector with the paper, wrapping it around to the back and securing with tape. ***Note:*** *For cookie sheets with raised edges, simply cut a piece of paper to fit the center section.* Cover the entire top surface of the paper with clear Contact paper or several laminating sheets.

3 Cut off another section of the paper that includes the same images as those on the covered metal sheet and back it with a piece of poster board or card stock. Cover with clear Contact. Cut out the images that match those that are on the covered metal sheet.

4 Attach a magnetic strip to the back of each. Make sure magnetic strips are firmly attached and cannot be easily pulled off. The object of the "game" is for little ones to match the magnetic figures to the same images on the covered board. ■

Paper Plus

Paper plus what? Could be acetate sheets, clockworks, a roll of cork, even a stone. There are many terrific crafts that don't call for paper as the main ingredient, but need paper to make them complete. That's what this chapter is all about. Two sheets of acetate turn into a practical dinner-table addition; a shopping bag is now part of your home decor; a roll of cork teamed with note cards becomes a gift for a friend; and the stone is now one you wouldn't think of throwing back. Once again, it's paper that makes it all happen.

Dear Suzie-
We had such a good time
at the lake with you and
Bob. We're still laughing
about our fish fry.
Can't wait to get together
again.

Cheers!
Melanie

Rock, Paper, Scissors

Rock, paper, scissors—remember that old kids' game? That game is the only other time I can ever remember putting those words together in the same sentence, but that's exactly what this project is all about … rock, paper and scissors. A bonus to this project is that a supply of stones is usually readily available … in the yard, along the beach, along the road or in nurseries. Obviously these are not only unusual, but very inexpensive, and they make wonderful surprise gifts.

Materials

Medium or large stones, washed clean

Tissue paper, handmade paper, ephemera, photocopies, etc.

Decorative embellishments such as wire, charms, jewels, etc.

Felt (optional)

Scissors

Flat paintbrush

Acrylic medium or white clear-drying glue

1 Brush a layer of acrylic medium or white glue onto top of stone. While the medium is wet, add torn paper pieces allowing paper edges to overlap; add any ephemera. Let dry.

2 Apply another layer of acrylic medium and let dry. Add any desired embellishments: wire, jewels, charms, buttons, etc. **Note:** *To protect furniture surfaces, adhere a piece of felt to the bottom of the stone.* ■

Art Stone

Paperweight Stone

Personal Stone

Gift Stone

Variations

Art Stone: This one's a rock! Painted with cream acrylic paint, it's decorated with an assortment of torn papers and rubber-stamped images, including one sprinkled with glitter. A strip of red-painted corrugated paper with accented gold-painted ridges was wrapped around rock, along with woven ribbon and fine wire. Beads and a charm were the final additions. This would make a nice gift.

Paperweight Stone: This stone was covered with elegant copper and gold leaf, then wrapped with wire. A tiny, wire-wrapped, polished stone adds the finishing touch.

Personal Stone: A collage of family photos was adhered to this stone. Then it was wrapped with fine-gauge wire and embellished with a small metal charm.

Gift Stone: Assorted papers and postage stamps were glued to this stone. Then it was tied around with several strands of black thread and accented with a small heart charm.

Changeable Place Mats

These place mats might never be used with your fine crystal and good silver at a dinner party, but for family meals they are perfect. We've used stickers, cutouts, photos and rubber stamps to decorate our mats. In most cases, we've used construction paper as the background, but wallpaper, gift-wrapping paper or double-sided card stock works well, too.

Materials

12 x 18-inch sheets of construction paper

12 x 18-inch sheets of clear acetate*

Colored plastic tape, crochet thread, yarn or sewing machine with all-purpose thread

Tapestry needle (if using crochet thread or yarn)

⅛-inch hole punch (if using yarn)

12 x 18-inch piece of cardboard (optional)

*Acetate can usually be purchased in 12 x 18-inch-sheet tablets or by the yard at art-supply stores.

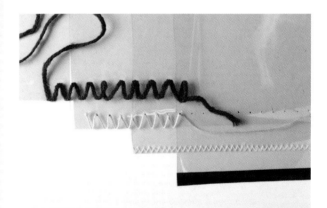

1 Select or cut two 12 x 18-inch sheets of acetate. On one piece sew an overcast stitch along one short end, placing the stitches about ½ inch apart and about ½ inch from the outside edge. If hand-sewing using crochet thread, it helps to use your needle to prepunch the holes. If using yarn, punch the holes using a small hole punch. If using a sewing machine, use a zigzag stitch. If using tape, cover the end of the acetate sheet by overlapping half of the width of the tape on each side.

2 Place the second sheet of acetate on top of the first and continue sewing or taping around the other three sides, this time sewing through or taping over both layers of the acetate to join them. The previously stitched or taped end remains open.

3 Trim the construction paper to fit inside your place mat before decorating.

Tip

To give the place mats more body, sandwich a 12 x 18-inch sheet of cardboard between two decorative sheets.

4 Slip in the decorated piece of paper. You can make the place mat reversible by decorating two sheets of paper and inserting them back to back or by using double-sided card stock as shown here. ∎

Coffee-Filter Flowers

This idea may sound silly, but the truth is there was a day when I used coffee filters for crafting because choices were limited and anything that even looked like paper was fair game. Those ruffled circles were perfect for making angels (you could decorate an entire Christmas tree with one pack of filters), flowers and party-favor parasols. When I recently saw them in a craft book used to make paper yo-yos, I was delighted. What I had once used out of necessity was now apparently considered a legitimate crafting material! So here they are … Coffee-Filter Flowers!

Materials

Round coffee filters:
white or tan, large or
small

Thread

Buttons and/or small
beads

Watercolor paints or food
coloring

Plastic trash bag or
dinner plate

Dish of water

Paper towels

Plastic gloves (optional)

Small paintbrush

Sewing needle

Scissors

1 Flatten a filter; fold it in half, then in half again and again.

2 Cut off about 1–1½-inch-wide band along the top ruffled edge. The remaining center circle will be the yo-yo. The band will be another flower.

3 Make a cut in the ruffled band, so you have one long strip and with needle and thread, take running stitches along the cut edge.

4 Gather into a circle and secure thread. Set aside for the moment.

5 Place the inner circle from step 2 on a dinner plate or on a spread-out trash bag. Using the paintbrush, "paint" the entire circle with water.

6 Start adding the color with watercolors or food coloring. Remember that the color you paint around the edge will be the center of the yo-yo and the inside color will be the outside or main color.

7 When the coloring is complete and while the filter is still wet, run the edge of the gathered flower from step 4 around the filter to pick up enough color to color the edge. Set aside.

8 Put filter flowers on a piece of paper towel to dry. Repeat entire process to make desired number of flowers.

9 When all the flowers are dry, turn the circles into yo-yos by taking a running stitch around the outside of each circle. Unlike the fabric yo-yos, there is no need to create a hem. When stitching is complete, carefully pull the thread to gather. Secure thread.

10 Once all of the blossoms are complete, use them to decorate boxes, journal covers, cards, scrapbook pages, etc. *Note: Buttons or beads can be adhered to flower centers.* ■

Options

Our journal has a torn piece of handmade paper topped with two yo-yo flowers and one gathered flower. The button centers have fibers threaded through them. The leaves and stems are cut from handmade paper and were adhered with gel medium. The flowers are held in place with double-sided tape.

Our wooden box was first painted with acrylic paint then decorated on top with three yellow and lavendar yo-yo flowers with seed-bead centers. A torn length of scrapbook paper is glued below the flowers.

This wooden frame was covered with wide strips torn from a brown grocery bag that were first crumpled, then flattened and stamped with a leaf design before being applied to the frame with gel medium. The stamping was done with permanent ink so it wouldn't run when the gel medium was applied. The yo-yo flower is embellished with small gold beads in the center. The stem and leaves were torn from a paper napkin and applied with the gel medium. More gold beads are applied randomly around the frame. A gold-leaf pen was used to highlight the inner and outer edges of the frame.

Chalk Marbleized Paper

Serious marbleizing is an art of its own. This almost instant method obviously is not, but I find it fascinating, and it is certainly a method that is open to experimentation with different papers, different color combinations and even different techniques. The first time I tried this method for marbleizing paper, I used card stock and made little boxes with it, but I really think this technique is better suited to making things like bookmarks, note cards, stationery and the like. In any case, it's still quick and easy, and certainly inexpensive. The youngsters might enjoy trying this as well.

Materials
140-lb watercolor paper*
Waxed paper
Colored chalk sticks or
  squares
Large cake pan or
  dishpan
Paring knife or craft knife
Iron

Watercolor paper is recommended, but not necessary.

Note
Surprisingly, the chalk will not rub off with normal use.

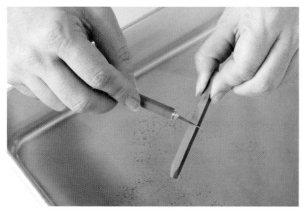

2 Using the sharp blade of a paring knife or craft knife, scrape the sides of various sticks of chalk in different but compatible colors over the water. Move your hands around as you scrape the chalk so you eventually have the surface reasonably covered with the fine shavings. You may choose to dip your paper at this point or you might swirl the water around a bit first.

1 Fill a dishpan or large cake pan with lukewarm water.

3 Carefully place the paper on top of the water, then just as carefully lift it up and off.

OR holding the piece of paper at one end, slowly and carefully slide the other end into the water until the entire piece is under water.

5 Place the marbled paper on a piece of waxed paper on a countertop. When completely dry, cover with a piece of waxed paper and press with a warm iron. Wait several hours before doing this or the chalk will spread, and the paper will be more inclined to curl. ■

4 Then just as carefully and slowly, pull it out again. This technique will color both sides. If you miss a spot, don't re-dip it. It usually doesn't work.

Things to Make

Note Cards & Envelopes— Note cards and envelopes can be made using the first (non-dipping) method. This works well by holding the cards open and placing just the front cover on the chalked water. Envelopes can be colored in the same way, holding the envelope by the flap.

Dear Suzie—
We had such a good time at the lake with you and Bob. We're still laughing about our fish fry.
Can't wait to get together again.

Cheers!
Melanie

Stationery—Ordinary copy paper was dipped, dried and ironed, and works well for stationery. The ironing smoothed out any wrinkles.

Quotes—
Famous & Otherwise

It seems everybody enjoys quotations ranging from philosophical musings to amusing one-liners. I've been collecting quotes for a number of years and finally decided to do something with them—make magnets and put them in this book. You might include one with a card, write them in a journal, or add them to a scrapbook. Or you might do what my friend Tavy Stone did many years ago: Make a scrapbook of quotations and give it to a friend. In this case, the friend was me.

Materials

Several quotations
Computer and printer
Pen and paper (optional)
Scrap paper
Frame rubber stamp
Ink pad
Colored pencils or
    markers
Ruler
Craft knife
Scanner
Peel-off magnetic
    sheeting or Xyron
    machine with magnetic
    cartridges
Tape

Tip

I used a home scanner for making my framed quotations. You could also go to your local copy shop. Any coloring is best done at the time you stamp the image.

1 Stamp an image of your selected frame on a scrap piece of paper. Color it, and cut out the frame and the center opening.

2 Select several favorite computer fonts and type one or more quotations in a variety of configurations. The size of the font will be determined by the size of the opening on your stamp. Print several samples of each quote, being certain to leave a good amount of space above and below each quote. ***Note:*** *You could also hand-print quotations on paper.*

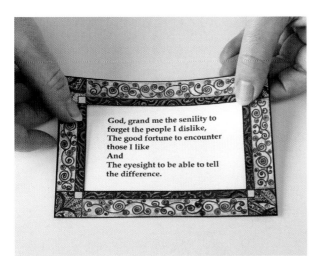

3 Place the cut-out frame on top of your printed copy to see if it will fit, and if it looks appropriate. If, by chance, the frame is rather large and the quote is too short, reduce the size of the frame before adding the quote.

4 Tape the selected copy to the back of the frame; scan it and print it out, or reduce the size and then print it out. I reduced all of mine at least once and often twice. Adhere frame to a piece of peel-off magnetic sheeting or run through a Xyron machine using a magnetic cartridge. ■

Sample Quotes

Wrinkled was not one of the things I wanted to be when I grew up.

Don't go around saying the world owes you a living. The world owes you nothing. It was here first.
~ Mark Twain

Housework never killed anyone, but why risk it?

I've got all the money I'll ever need ... unless I buy something.

I always wanted to be somebody, but I should have been more specific. ~ Lily Tomlin

DEFINITION
Multitasking: Messing everything up at the same time.

Some days it's all Baltic Avenue.

If you don't care where you are, you ain't lost.

THE MAIN THING IS TO KEEP THE MAIN THING, THE MAIN THING.
~ Albert Einstein

The woman who says that money doesn't buy happiness just doesn't know where to shop.
~ Bo Derek

The road to a friend's house is always short.

Clock in a Bag

This is one of those "who would have thought?" projects that can become addictive in no time. It was my friend Linda Watson who made the wonderful two-sided, two-clock bag (see page 114) some time ago, but I never tried making one until this book. After buying about 10 bags in different colors, different sizes and different patterns, I decided the best bet would be to simply take a plain bag and add my own designs. Once you see the basic directions, you can decide to design your own or find that absolutely perfect bag, as Linda did.

Materials

Colorful gift bag (heavy-weight paper preferred)

Paper design of choice (cut from photo, note card, calendar, etc.)

Clockworks and hands and/or small clock insert

Adhesive-backed clock numerals

¼-inch-thick piece of foam board

Ribbon or cord

Desired embellishments (scrapbook paper, fringe, etc.)

Japanese screw punch or knitting needle for puncturing hole in foam board

Paper punch

Decorative-edge scissors

Removable tape

Double-sided adhesive

Hook-and-loop tape (optional)

1 Open bag and observe the creases. There will be at least one crease across one side. Consider this the back of the bag.

2 Decide on any desired trim or design. If you will be adding a cut-out design or a picture, place it in position on the front of the bag with removable tape to determine where the clockworks will be placed. Punch out or carefully poke a hole for the center shaft on the clockworks, going through the hole and the front of the bag only.

Tip

For added security against tearing, you might wish to put a piece of tape over the punch-out area on the inside before making the hole.

3 Measure the width and the height of the bag, measuring to just under the holes for the handle. Cut two pieces of foam board slightly smaller in both directions and insert in the bag, placing a piece in both the front and the back of the bag. With a sharp object or a pencil point, mark through the hole on the front of the bag onto the foam piece to indicate where the clock shaft will go.

4 Remove the foam piece and drill a hole through the foam in this spot.

5 Carefully remove handles. If the handles were taped in place so there are no holes, punch two holes in the top portion. These will be for the ribbon.

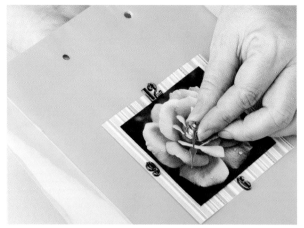

6 Flatten the bag on your work surface and add your desired trim and embellishments to the front. Our green bag has two stacked rectangles: the striped scrapbook paper and the smaller, center photograph of a rose. Add the clock numerals around the center photograph.

Open bag and return foam pieces to the inside. Attach them to the inside using strips of double-sided adhesive along the top and bottom edges.

7 Insert and assemble the clockworks following the directions on the package. Don't forget the batteries.

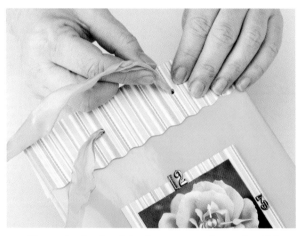

8 Close the bag. If desired, you may put a strip of hook-and-loop tape across the bag to give a bit of dimension to this area. For the top, cut a piece of scrapbook paper the width of the bag and twice as deep as you want it to be, plus ¼ inch. Our top measures 7⅟₁₆ x 3¾ inches deep on each side plus the ¼-inch strip running down the center. Score and fold along each side of the ¼-inch space in the center. Trim along the width edges with decorative-edge scissors.

9 From the back of the bag, insert the ends of the ribbon through the two holes and tie the bow in the front. ■

Tip
Put a handful of glass stones or a sealable plastic bag filled with unpopped popcorn in the bag to give it some weight.

Notes on Bags in General

Every once in a while you will find a bag that appears to be made exactly for this project. There are bags with large polka dots or gigantic flowers that seem perfect for clock inserts. One from Grand Central Station that has "It's time for Grand Central" printed on it certainly seems to have been made for a real-life clock to be inserted. Once you start looking, you may end up, as I did, with a box full of bags that seem just perfect for turning into clocks. And if I never get to them, I still have a bunch of great bags for gift wrapping.

Viewer Frankee Migliorisi wrote that she turned a bunch of Christmas shopping bags into clocks that she also filled with small gifts. Into the bags went inexpensive soft toys along with some wooden toys her husband had made. Frankee also made seven of them for special friends. I'm guessing that the children got the toys, and the moms and dads got the clocks for holiday decorations.

Two-Sided Clock in a Bag

I don't know which came first—the bag or the idea—but in any case this bag looks like a natural. On one side, Linda put the workings for a clock as described for our green bag, with no need to add any embellishments. The setting was already there.

On the other side, she cut out the circle in the design just large enough for the clock insert. The clock insert is nestled in a 3 x 3-inch piece of foam board with a circle cut in the middle of it. Before attaching the foam to the bag, the clock insert was removed, the foam was attached to the bag and the clock insert was re-inserted from the front of the bag into the foam. It all appears to have been made that way.

Refrigerator Puzzles

If competition for refrigerator display space isn't a problem in your house, these big square puzzles might be a fun thing to add. Most of the puzzles I've seen are made with 4-inch squares, though smaller squares would be a bit more of a challenge in less space. I was totally delighted when I saw how beautifully a number of my 4 x 6-inch snapshots took to enlarging. They all looked so great, I'm either going to have to get a larger refrigerator or think up more projects.

Materials

Enlarged photograph or picture
  of choice from a calendar
Self-stick mounting board or
  sturdy cardboard*
Laminating sheet or clear
  Contact paper (optional)
Pen
Craft knife and cutting mat,
  or paper cutter
Ruler
Roll of magnetic tape
Adhesive of choice

*Self-stick mounting boards come in
different sizes at your local craft store or
you can use a piece of cardboard and either
a spreadable or a spray-on adhesive.

Photo Credit

My thanks to my friend and neighbor, Susie Thomas for the beautiful snapshot she took of a sunset over Lake Michigan.

Note: Since I already had several pieces of 9 x 12-inch cardboard, as well as the same size self-stick mounting board, I opted for 3-inch squares, since these would require no trimming. Should you prefer to go all out on a larger picture or smaller squares, the basic directions remain the same. Only the math changes.

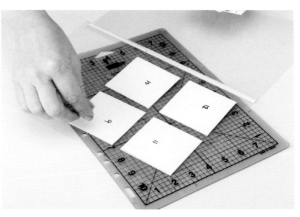

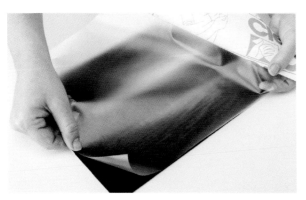

1 Adhere the desired-size picture to a self-stick mounting board and cover with a laminating sheet.

Note: If you feel that working with a large piece of laminating sheet or contact paper is a bit tricky to deal with, wait until after cutting the squares (steps 2, 3) and apply them individually to smaller sheets of the laminating material and cut them out one at a time. That's what I finally did.

2 Determine the size squares you want. For a 9 x 12 inch horizontal picture you will have:

• 4-inch squares = 3 across, 2 down = total 6 squares - trim picture 1 inch across the bottom

• 3-inch squares = 4 across, 3 down = total 12 squares - no trimming required

• 2-inch squares = 6 across, 4 down = total 24 squares - trim picture 1 inch across the bottom

• 1-inch squares = 12 across, 9 down = total 108 squares - no trimming required

3 Cut the squares with a paper cutter, or if cutting by hand, turn the picture over and mark the cardboard into squares.

4 Cut out using a sharp-bladed craft knife and a ruler. Be certain to number the squares as you go, so you will know how to put it back together again.

5 Depending on the size of your squares, add one or two small pieces of magnetic tape, or a piece of magnetic sheeting to the back of each piece and mount them on the refrigerator … or a filing cabinet … or any other metal surface that is handy and big enough. Make it a game to see who can be the first one to assemble the pieces. ■

This calendar photo of a Claude Monet painting looked like it would be a serious challenge no matter what size squares were cut. I had it copied on 80 lb. paper and after adhering it to an adhesive backed mounting board I cut it into 1 inch squares! I made sure to number the pieces on the back, but I did not cover it with a laminating sheet.

Note Card Coasters

This is another of my favorite projects, and one that I can honestly say I have used for years. A four-piece set of these coasters makes a terrific gift, because in addition to being practical, it can be personalized. I have a set featuring some wonderful winter photographs as well as some taken at the beach. You are in no way limited to using note cards and photos. Greeting cards and calendars are also great sources for terrific pictures. Add the fact that these are easy and inexpensive to make, and you've got a winner.

Materials

Cork, either precut or in rolls

Pictures of choice: photographs, greeting cards, calendar pictures, etc.

Rubber cement or Xyron machine adhesive cartridge

Craft knife

4-inch square mini ruler, standard ruler, or 4-inch square of cardboard

Laminating sheets, or Xyron machine with laminating cartridge

Sheet of card stock or lightweight cardboard for cutting template

Project notes: Cork is sometimes available in sheets or precut shapes at your craft store. Because I couldn't find any precut shapes when I was looking, all of my coasters are made with cork that I purchased in 12 x 36 x 1/16-inch rolls at the hardware store. It meant gluing two or more layers together to get the thickness I wanted, but that was easy enough to do.

The directions given use glue and laminating sheets applied by hand, but you can also use a laminating machine with an adhesive/laminating cartridge. The cork goes through easily.

1 Cut a 4-inch square out of the center of a piece of card stock or lightweight cardboard (a paper plate works great!) to use as a template. Position the template over your selected pictures to determine which portion of the picture to use. Draw around the template with a sharp pencil.

Using a ruler and craft knife, cut out the selected picture. Cut out three more for a total of four.

2 If you are using cork that comes in a roll, you will need to flatten it out. To do this, cut off a 4½- to 5-inch-wide strip and cut it into squares. Don't worry about measuring exactly or cutting with a knife and ruler at this point. Scissors will do. It will still curl. Following the directions on the rubber-cement container for the most permanent adhesion, apply a coat of the cement to the inside of two of the curled pieces.

3 Allow to dry and press the two surfaces together. Because they will be curling against each other, this will flatten them. After they are completely set, you may wish to add another layer of cork, although this is not necessary.

4 Apply adhesive to your selected picture and press to the top of the stacked-and-glued cork piece. When adhesive is set, use a ruler and craft knife to trim the cork to match the picture. Be certain the blade is sharp. Cut slowly.

5 Laminate the top surface with either a laminating sheet or run it through the Xyron. Trim the laminate to fit. Done! ∎

Note

Of course, just *after* I had my set completed, I found a package of cork mats at my craft store! They were round and ¼-inch thick and would be perfect for this project. No gluing is needed for these, but either method works.

Option: To curve the corners use your craft knife to cut off the corners at an angle. Cut off only a very small portion then soften the cut edges with an emery board. Do this before adding the laminating sheet.

Greeting Card Photo Credit

My thanks to Melanie Parke, a northern Michigan artist, who gave me permission to use her cards for my coasters. Melanie had the cards made from one of her oil paintings.

Show-Offs

Show-offs! Every family has them, and I'm not referring to the 6-year-old or the teenager or the family member who thinks they are the cutest or the funniest or the cleverest. I'm referring to all those pictures you've taken of the 6-year-old and the teenager and the family member. You do have them, I'm sure … along with all the other photos you've taken to remind you of special moments, special people and special times. And because they are special, let's not limit them to albums or shoe boxes or memory sticks. Let's get them out and spread the joy. That's what this chapter is all about—showing off those pictures in greeting-card frames, on box tops, on the refrigerator or in cards to send. We're a country of picture takers. Let's show them off!

Never-Ending Card

When Cherryl showed me this seemingly complicated card that you just keep unfolding, and then demonstrated to me how ridiculously easy it is to make—I couldn't believe it. Of course I loved it and couldn't wait to make one myself. I used photographs. Cherryl rubber stamped hers. Mine was a mini-scrapbook of a fun weekend. Cherryl stamped a thank you card. But what about making a birth announcement, or party invitations, or table favors for a bridal shower? A national hamburger chain used these cards to promote a movie. A local car dealership advertised its new models. Join the crowd.

Materials

Lightweight white or light-color card stock	Ruler
	Scissors
Pen or pencil	Bone folder
Rubber stamps, photos, etc.	Glue or glue stick

Project notes: These never-ending cards can be almost any size, as long as the length of the original four rectangles is twice as long as the width, such as 3 x 6 inches, 4 x 8 inches, 6 x 12 inches, etc.

When telling a story with photographs, don't forget to leave blank spaces for journaling.

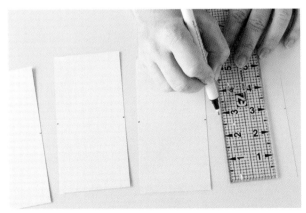

1 Cut four 3 x 6-inch rectangles from card stock. Mark dots at the center of the long sides on each rectangle.

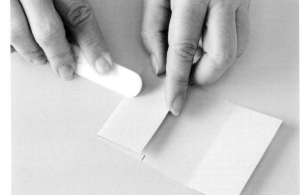

2 Fold the ends of each rectangle to the center and crease well; unfold.

3 Place two rectangles side by side vertically on the work surface.

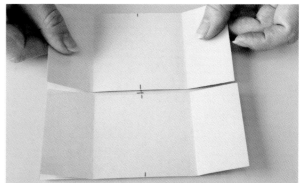

4 Place the remaining two rectangles horizontally on top of the first two. Position rectangles so that all outside edges match as closely as possible, and so that the two inside edges do not overlap.

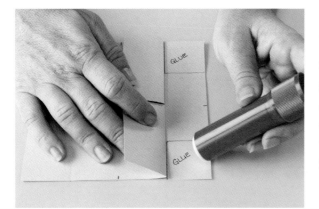

5 Glue just the four corner areas together as indicated by fold lines.

6 Once glue is dry, open the card and re-crease along all four folds. Open the card again and re-crease all visible folds. Open two more times to get back to the beginning. *Note: At this point, it may be necessary to trim the edges for a perfect fit.* If desired, cut off corners in a decorative design. Cherryl left the corners of her card as is. I cut the outside corners in a curve.

7 Begin to decorate the card, deciding how much of each image will show at each progressive opening. A paper model of the card can be made following steps 1–5 to help visualize. ∎

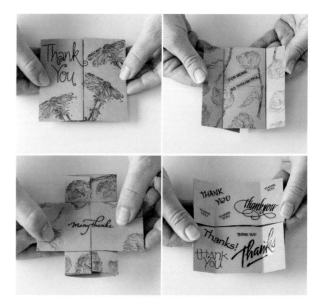

Here's How It Works

This card looks very complicated, but it's amazingly simple to make. This series of photos shows how the folds look at each stage in the process. The photos on the left show an undecorated sample, while the photos on the right show a completed card.

Photo 1
The front of the card.

Photo 2
Open the vertical flaps to reveal the horizontal flaps.

Photo 3
Open top and bottom middle flaps, revealing vertical flaps.

Photo 4
Open side flaps to reveal the last layer of photos. Open top and bottom flaps, and you're back at the beginning! *Note: After making our cards to have them open horizontally (step 4) we turned them so they opened vertically. It's your choice. Try them both ways before you decorate. I managed to put 23 different photographs on my card. You might do more … or not.*

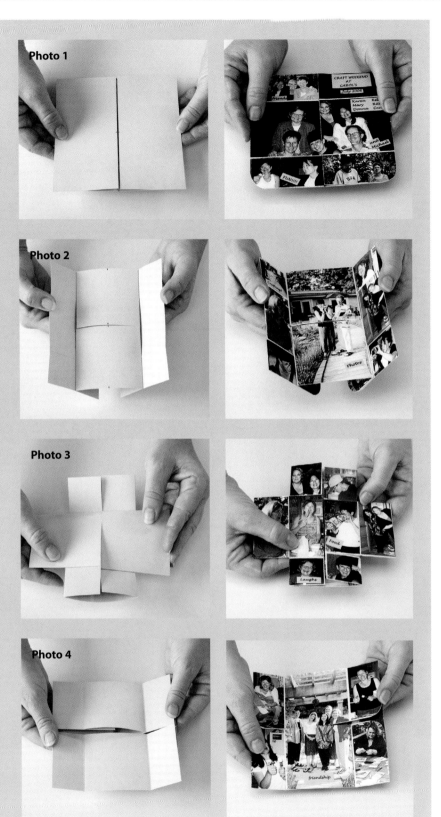

Photo 1

Photo 2

Photo 3

Photo 4

Stamp & Fold Frames

These little paper frames might never make it to the top of the grand piano, but in a bookcase, bedroom or any casual setting, they are perfectly at home. The really good news is that these are not only nice-looking, and easy and inexpensive to make, but there are so many frame stamps out there in different sizes, shapes and styles that you can certainly find one or more especially for your tastes.

Materials

Photograph
140-lb watercolor paper
Frame rubber stamp
Embossing ink
Gold embossing powder
Embossing heat tool
Ruler
Craft knife
Glue
Piece of acetate
  (optional)

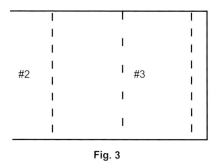

Fig. 1

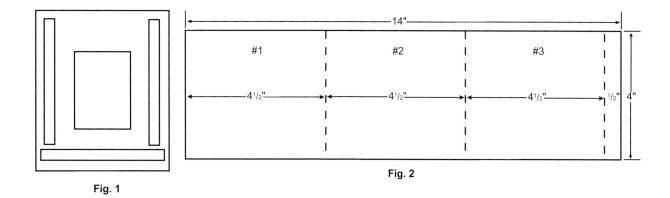

Fig. 2

Project note: *Our stamped image measures 3¾ inches wide and 4¼ inches high. I added a small border to bring the final measurements to 4 x 4½ inches. You should measure your stamped image and adjust the following measurements accordingly.*

1 Stamp frame image on watercolor paper, emboss and wait until the melted powder has completely cooled. Cut out. Depending on the stamped image, you may elect to add borders inside and out as pictured.

2 Cut three strips of the watercolor paper to ½ inch wide and 4 inches long. Glue to the back of the frame along the two outside edges and along the bottom edge (Fig. 1).

3 Put the frame aside for a moment and cut a length of the watercolor paper 4 inches wide by 14 inches long (three times the height plus ½ inch). Score at 4½-inch intervals. You should have a ½-inch flap left over (Fig. 2).

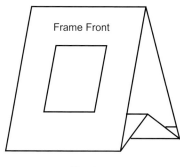

Fig. 3

Fig. 4

4 Fold along all scored lines in the same direction so the piece forms a triangle (see Fig. 4). Flatten piece again, turn it over and score another line across the middle of section #3 (Fig. 3). Turn piece back to original position.

5 Glue the watercolor-paper strips on the frame to section #2 of the folded paper with the top open end of the frame facing section #1.

6 Again fold paper into the triangle and glue the ½-inch flap to the inside of section #1. Push up along the scored line in section #3 (Fig. 4).

7 Insert photo. Cover photo with a piece of acetate to enhance appearance, if desired. ■

Look Who's Talking

These magnetic talking pictures are really fun. You can buy them in gift shops, card shops, novelty shops and drugstores, but it's more fun to make your own. Go searching through your old photographs and those of the kids; match them up with appropriate or inappropriate sayings that you can find in magazines or write them yourself. Then put them on the refrigerator for all to see.

Materials

Photographs or
  photocopies
Magnetic sheeting*
Laminating sheets*
Construction paper or
  card stock
Glue stick
Scissors

Bone folder (optional)
Quotations (your own, or
  those of other people,
  or headlines from the
  paper or magazines)
A sense of humor

If you have a Xyron with a magnetic sheet/laminate cartridge, this is the project for it.

1 Select and cut out photos. Leave a small border all the way around, if desired.

2 Type, print and cut out an appropriate saying, or look through newspapers and magazines for a saying that might fit.

3 Glue the photo to a piece of construction paper or card stock along with the selected words. Attach the entire piece to a piece of magnetic sheeting and cover the front with a piece of laminate. Rub with bone folder to insure a smooth adhesion.

4 Cut out as pictured, leaving a slight border all the way around. ∎

Greeting Card Frames

A viewer sent this idea to me a number of years ago, and I still think it is one of the quickest-to-make projects I've seen. As you may have guessed from the title, all of the frames pictured were made by cutting out the center of a note card or a greeting card. What could be easier? Many Christmas cards already contain a frame in their design. Those are naturals.

Materials

Note cards and greeting cards
Piece of cardboard or paper
Metal-edged ruler
Craft knife
Pencil
Double-sided tape
Small piece of card stock (for easel)

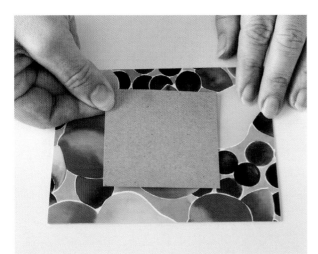

1 It helps to visualize how a card will look as a frame by cutting a piece of cardboard or paper to represent the cutout. When you have the desired size, cut around it using a ruler and craft knife.

2 Place photo behind cutout and tape in place. Tape card closed on three sides using double-sided tape.

3 Make a small easel by cutting a triangle out of another card or a piece of card stock. Fold one side back ½ inch and tape it to the back of the card. Cut the bottom edge at a slight angle and cut off the point at the top. ∎

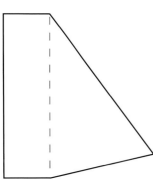

Greeting Card Frames
Easel

Tip

To add a nice touch, cut a mat of a complementary color. The beach scene has a very small border of pink cut from card stock.

Photo Credits

To give credit where credit is due, I should mention that the attractive children are Kitty Bartholomew's son and daughters … Bo, Birdie and Brooke. The picture was taken long enough ago to embarrass all three of them. The flower picture is mine, and the beautiful cat is Roka, twin brother of Olive who is equally as black and beautiful. They belong to Michael and Rita Duvall, although I'm not sure that it's not the other way around. Michael is the photographer.

Picture-Topped Shaker Boxes

Practical, pretty and quick as a wink to decorate, these little balsa-wood, shaker-style boxes have been a staple in most craft stores since forever and with good reason. They can so easily be decorated and used for everything from gift boxes to tabletop decorations to tree ornaments. I've put my personal photographs on the top of my boxes, but cutouts from greeting cards or note cards, or your own artwork also works well. Once you get started, you won't want to stop. These make nice little gifts even without putting anything inside them.

Materials

Small balsa wood or papier-mâché box

Picture for top of box— personal photo, note card, calendar photo, etc.

Paper for making templates

Ribbon, beaded fringe, etc.

Marker (optional)

Acrylic paint

Paintbrush

Small sharp scissors

Craft knife

Pencil with sharp point

Adhesives of choice

Project note: I have used photographs printed on glossy paper. If you prefer to use photocopies, it is best to laminate the picture before attaching it to the box. A laminate/adhesive cartridge would do both jobs at once.

1 Place the box top upside down on a piece of paper, draw around it and cut it out. Use this as a template to select the exact portion of any picture you want to use. Draw around the cutout using a very sharp pencil. Cut out the shape, cutting on the drawn line.

2 Before attaching the picture to the box top, paint the sides of the top and the entire box in a color to coordinate with the picture. You might also wish to color the edge of the picture to make the white edge less obvious.

3 When the paint is dry, attach the picture to the box top. If any of the picture extends beyond the edge of the box top, cut it off using either a craft knife or scissors with a thin blade. Cuticle scissors are excellent for this.

4 Add trim if desired. Our boxes have ribbon or beaded fringe around the sides of the box tops. ■

Tip

When cutting with scissors to cut a curved shape, remember to move the paper into the scissors and take small cuts. To avoid stop and start marks, do not ever close the point of the scissors.

Personality Frames

One of the best things about decorating these unique frames is that there are no rules—lots of suggestions but no rules. They don't even have to hold a photograph! It can be any picture or drawing that will have meaning to the recipient. If you are a purist and still believe that the word unique means "one of a kind," these frames are indeed unique because each one is personalized for one person. That alone should make it a perfect gift.

Materials

Frame with wide border

Mat board

Paint

Fine-grit sandpaper

Brown paper bag
  (optional)

Appropriate adhesive

White glue or decoupage
  adhesive

Protective finish

Assortment of pictures,
  charms/mementos

Project notes: *The frame should have a flat or slightly curved border at least 1½ inches wide. Craft stores, frame stores, antique stores and yard sales are good sources. I actually obtained two of mine from my neighbor's trash!*

Before You Start

Preparation for making one of these frames usually begins long before you start putting it together. After deciding for whom you will be making the frame, list all of their characteristics, hobbies, interests, likes, dislikes, etc., that you can think of. What you don't know, you can find out.

1 Start collecting pictures of things you have on your list that represent what the person is about. Look through magazines, catalogs and travel brochures. Cut out and save all that you find in an envelope. If a picture is too large, you can have it reduced. Use snapshots or portions of snapshots in the same way. Also consider using stickers and small items such as charms and miniature dimensional pieces. If possible, gather souvenirs such as ticket stubs, paper napkins, swizzle sticks, etc.

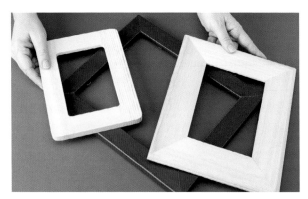

2 Prepare the frame by sanding, painting or staining, then lightly sanding again. When sanding after painting, use a very fine (600-grit) wet/dry sandpaper or a piece of brown paper bag.

3 Glue on all the selected paper items using an appropriate adhesive. Before adding dimensional items, apply a protective coating to the paper-covered frame.

4 When dry, add the dimensional items.

The dimensional items on our "Crafty Friend" frame include a pair of scissors, a swatch of knitting done on skewers then cut to size, a bottle of glitter, a plastic canvas embroidered heart done on 14-count canvas, some embroidery floss, a pile of beads, a tiny card stamped with a very small rubber stamp, a small wooden heart indicating that the frame was made for "My Crafty Friend." When you've finished embellishing the frame, insert the selected picture. In this case it is a photo of the crafty friend crafting. ∎

Linda's Frames

To help get you going, following are several descriptions of other frames, and the stories of how they got started.

The first time I saw one of these personalized frames was when my dear and talented friend Linda Watson made and gave one of them to a co-worker when we both worked on *The Home Show*. From then on, her services were constantly in demand. Every time somebody knew somebody who was having a birthday, anniversary or celebration of some sort, the request went out to Linda to make a frame "for so-and-so who loves such-and-such." I caught the fever and made a few myself. I must admit that, though they take a bit of time and planning ahead, they really are a kick to make. The feeling of satisfaction you get after making one makes every bit of time spent well worth it. Don't wait for a special event to make one—any gift-giving occasion is the perfect time.

• For a friend who collected Marilyn Monroe memorabilia, Linda decorated a frame with a single picture of the star that she reduced and printed over and over again; then she covered the entire frame with these copies. The frame itself contained one large photo of Miss Monroe.

• Any Beatles fan would consider the Beatles frame that Linda made to be priceless. It is covered with pictures of the Beatles that were taken from newspapers, sheet music, magazines and some from sources I can't even imagine. There is even a ticket to one of their concerts in Philadelphia dated Aug. 16, 1966, and in the middle of it all, a picture, of course, of the Beatles.

• One of my prized possessions is a frame Linda made for me covered with pictures of craft-book covers cut from ads, video tapes and photos of craft projects. She was even able to obtain a picture of the cover of a book that contained pictures of my son's artwork. There are a number of 3-D items including a tiny ball of yarn, some miniature knitting needles, a pair of scissors, a spool of thread and a pincushion. In the picture area was a drawing of a cartoon pig munching on a potato chip with his hand (hoof) in a can of chocolate-covered potato chips and a can of diet soda at his feet. Anyone who knew Linda knew that she existed on diet soda, chocolate and potato chips. If she could combine the two and get chocolate-covered potato chips, she was absolutely in pig-out heaven. It's priceless.

• The first frame that I made was for friend Peter Greenburg who was the travel reporter for *The Home Show* at the time. This was fun because I was able to obtain so many wonderful images from travel brochures, as well as from magazines and catalogs. There were pictures of countries, modes of transportation, highway signs, tickets and luggage labels. I also included a couple of miniaturized copies of snapshots I had taken of him and members of the cast when the show had gone on location. I ran out of space before I ran out of things to put on it. In the center was a matted photo of all of us from the show.

Cherryl's dog Osa framed by dogs

Jacob's Ladder Photo Folder

I was 10 years old when my father first taught me how to make a Jacob's Ladder, and they soon became my first business venture. I sold them door to door for 10 cents apiece and paid for half of my first big two-wheeler. I've been making them in various versions ever since. Jane Beard taught us this one using photographs, and by combining her directions with my father's method and a few suggestions from Cherryl, I think we have concocted the easiest method yet!

Materials

1½- to 2-inch circle or square paper punch

Two 4-inch squares of heavy chipboard or mat board

Four 4-inch squares of card stock

Six 2½-inch squares complementary card stock

26 inches ¼-inch-wide ribbon

Six photos to fit in punch-out shapes

Craft knife

Ruler

Glue stick or double-stick tape

Stamp pad or marker complementary to 4-inch squares of card stock (optional)

1 Punch or cut out openings in all six of the smaller card-stock squares to frame the photos, and tape or glue the photos to the back sides of these pieces.

2 Color the edges of the two 4-inch squares of chipboard with stamp pad or marker (optional). Glue a 4-inch square of the card stock to one side of each of the 4-inch chipboard squares. Glue a framed photo to the center of each of the two chipboard squares. These will be photos No. 1 and No. 6, the front and back of the folder.

3 Turn the chipboard pieces over, photo side down. Cut ribbon into four 6½-inch lengths. Glue or tape the ribbon to one of the chipboard squares as pictured, about 1 inch in from the outside edges. The top and bottom ribbons should be positioned ½ inch from the top and bottom edges of the board. The center ribbons can be anywhere from ⅛ inch (see main photo) to ¾ inch (above) apart (Fig. 1, page 143).

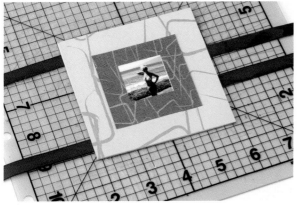

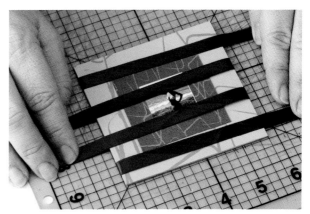

4 Turn chipboard piece over photo side up.

5 Bring the ribbons over the front of the chipboard (Fig. 2).

6 With photo side facing down, place the second piece of chipboard on top of the first. The ribbons are now sandwiched between the two pieces of chipboard with the ribbon ends extending about 1 inch beyond the edges (Fig. 3a).

Bring the ends back over the top piece of chipboard, pull taut and glue or tape the ends to secure (Fig. 3b).

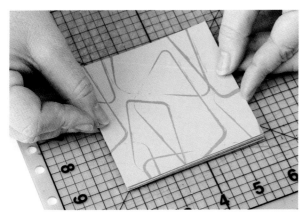

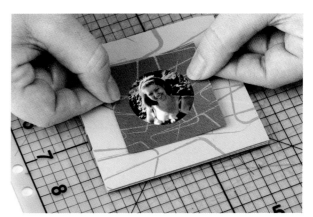

7 Glue or tape a cardstock square to both the top and bottom chipboard squares.

8 Attach a framed photo in the center of each square.

9 Open the cover of the folder so the two center strips of ribbon are on the right side. Slip a framed photo wrong side up under the two ribbons positioning it over the photo that is already there.

10 Attach the last framed photo right side up on top of this photo, sandwiching the ribbons between. All three photos are stacked on top of each other, but you should only see the one on the top.

11 You should now be able to open your folder from either the right or left side, no matter which way you close it, and see all six pictures. ∎

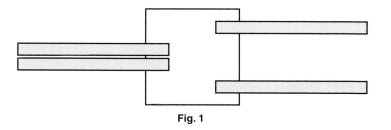

Fig. 1

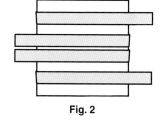

Fig. 2

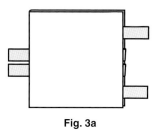

Fig. 3a

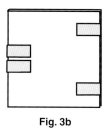

Fig. 3b

Art in Miniature

It seems that every family with grade-school children has a forever-changing collection of artwork brought home from school. I don't know when the trend of displaying those masterpieces on the refrigerator first started—probably when iceboxes moved from the back hall into the kitchen. Once that clean, uncluttered space became a display wall, there was no turning back. When there are brothers and sisters to contend with, equal display space can be a problem. No more. The problem has been solved, and all you need is your camera and a sheet of peel-off magnetic sheeting.

Materials

SLR or digital camera

Peel-off adhesive-backed
   magnetic sheeting

Scissors

Child's artwork

1 Place drawing on the floor.

2 With SLR or digital camera, stand over the drawing and take a picture. Take several from slightly different distances to get the size you desire.

3 Cut out the printed picture in the chosen size, place it on a piece of magnetic sheeting, trim the sheeting to fit the picture, and you're done. A school year's worth of art can go up there before you cover the entire door! Everybody's happy. Next year, it all starts over.

PS. At this size you can even carry a few artistic creations in your wallet! ■

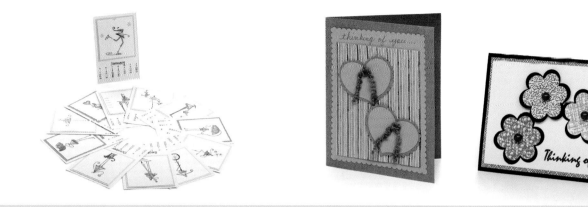

From the Shoe Box

One of the consistently favorite segments on *The Carol Duvall Show* over the years was the "Shoe Box" segment. It had nothing to do with shoes and at times nothing to do with a shoe box either. This was a segment when I read letters and ideas that the viewers had sent to me. Often they sent in the actual project they had made; more often they sent in photographs, and sometimes, they also included step-by-step directions. We received contributions from 3-year-olds (with mother's help) to 83-year-olds. As you can imagine, they covered a wide range of subject matter. Some were practical tips, some were extremely inventive, all were fascinating; but for this chapter, for this book, I have selected only the suggestions that viewers sent in that have to do with paper, card stock or cardboard. Chances are you will find an idea that will either help you, or inspire you or amuse you, or all three. I hope so.

What Kind of Photographs You Need ...

Either matte or glossy photos can be used. We used glossy; Roberta mixed both. Roberta found that pictures that had been printed on Fuji paper worked the best as far as resisting blistering when embossing. We found other papers such as Kodak can be used, but are much more sensitive to the heat and extra care should be taken. Experiment first. We used several kinds of paper.

Mosaic Photo Cards

I was totally taken with the mosaic photo cards sent to me by viewer Roberta James of Las Cruces, N.M. Thanks to the wonderfully detailed instructions that Roberta included, I was able to demonstrate how to make them on one of our shows. I thought a box of several of these cards would be a wonderful gift. They are handsome, unusual and rich-looking, yet inexpensive to make. Time is what they take, not money.

Materials

Several "bad" photographs

Card stock

Envelopes to match

Sticker paper or label paper

Large sheet of paper

Several assorted rubber stamps

Black permanent ink pad

Embossing powders in colors of choice

Heat gun

Ruler

Craft knife

Self-healing cutting mat

Tweezers

Glue stick

If you have taken snapshots the old-fashioned way with a film camera, I'm quite sure you have a number of pictures in your collection that are simply not album worthy. They are the kind of pictures you delete on your digital camera. They might be slightly out of focus, or boring, or perhaps you took too many at the same time and place. In any case, for this project you want what might be considered bad photos.

Same photo turned upside down and stamped over.

Note: You will be rubber-stamping on these photos, so at least some of them should have some open spaces in lighter colors, so that stamped images can be seen. The more color in the photos, the more color in the finished cards.

1 Stamp one or more images on the photos, stamping in any direction. You will want to cover most of the picture, because you are disguising the image beneath. ***Note:*** *Select one image to be the focal piece on your card. Unlike the other stamped images, you will want this image to be recognized.*

2 Using a ruler, craft knife and self-healing cutting mat, cut the photos into strips of varying widths not exceeding 1 inch. Cut the photo selected as the focal piece larger than the others.

3 Cut the strips into squares, rectangles and triangles to create mosaic pieces. Sort according to color.

4 Cut label/sticker paper sheet into a 3¾ x 5-inch piece. Peel and place sheet on work surface, sticky side up. Try not to touch the surface, with your fingers (tweezers are helpful!). Place the focal piece onto the sticky paper in the desired position. Leave room around it to add mosaic pieces on all four sides.

5 Arrange mosaic pieces in a pleasing manner around the focal image and continue to fill in the entire sticky paper, allowing about ⅛ inch between each of the pieces for the "grout." Do not worry if the pieces spill over the outside edges. When all mosaic pieces have been positioned, cut off the extending edges.

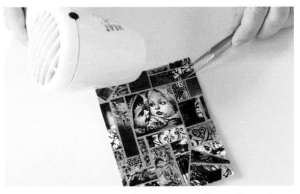

6 Place piece on a large piece of paper and sprinkle on embossing powder, taking care to generously cover all of the open areas.

7 Shake off excess embossing powder and use heat gun to emboss.

8 When piece is completed, use a glue stick to attach it to card stock cut to 4 x 5¼ inches. Attach assembled piece to a folded note card cut approximately ¼ inch larger on all sides. ■

Note: *This is the tricky part. Whether you are using a low- or a high-heat gun, hold it farther away from the paper than you usually do and at an angle. You want to emboss the powder, but you do not want to bubble the photo. It is recommended that you practice this technique before making any cards. If you do get a small bubble, all is not lost. Cover it with a charm! Notice the dragonfly?*

And Then ...

We boxed several cards in a small gift box which we had painted a compatible color, and then glued a photocopy of one of the cards to the top of the box. Only a ribbon was needed to complete the gift presentation.

Crafting With Envelope Linings

Viewer Martha Sanders Inks of Powell, Ohio, realized that many times the linings of the envelopes that her bills come in have fascinating patterns. By adding a few more lines made with colored markers, she created a whole new crafting material. It was just plain fun! The directions are easy, they cost you nothing, and the possibilities are endless.

Materials

A variety of envelopes with decorative linings from bills, junk mail, solicitations, etc.

Card stock in assorted colors

Felt-tipped pens in different widths and colors

Sentiment stamps

Ink pads

Scallop-edge scissors

Assorted punches

Ruler

Red beads

Fibers of your choice

Adhesive dimensional dots

Paper adhesive

Before

After

1 Cut open envelopes and press them flat. Draw a variety of straight lines in different directions using both wide- and narrow-tipped pens in a variety of colors.

2 Cut or punch the results into different shapes—rectangles, squares, circles, etc.—and use to decorate scrapbook pages, note cards and stationery. Use large pieces as backgrounds. Try layering some pieces. ■

Envelope Lining Card Creations

Make a card from medium blue card stock and top with a sage-green piece of card stock cut with scallop-edge scissors. Top with a sheet of envelope lining that has been colored with light blue, sage green, yellow and dark blue markers. Punch out and layer hearts in the same manner as for card. Cut two lengths of yarn, knot in the center and glue to the hearts for a finishing touch. A written sentiment will say it all.

Fold a piece of golden card stock in half and top with a piece of red, then white card stock. Adhere balloon shapes punched from colored, striped lining paper and add strings; stamp "Happy Birthday" to make the card complete.

For a layered card, start with the basic card in chocolate brown, top it with a slightly smaller piece of black, top the black piece with a dramatic background made of colored envelope lining. Three stamped images complete the rather dramatic-looking card.

Punch out gray and white lining paper flowers with paper punch or die cutter. Layer onto black card stock and cut around. Center each flower with a red pony bead. Attach flowers to layered card wtih dimensional adhesive dots.

ABC Book

Viewer Connie Anatra of Pembroke Pines, Fla., sent in this simple and clever idea. Connie took the "A is for apple" idea, cut out many pictures from magazines, catalogs, etc. Next, she divided them by letters of the alphabet, and glued them to pieces of card stock. Then she slipped them into one of those inexpensive little photo albums. Each page is a different letter.

This creative learning toy is small enough for a little one to handle easily. The pages are all protected with plastic sleeves that can be quickly wiped clean. The inserts can be personalized according to the child's ability, and it cost almost nothing to make. Fabulous!

Punched Paper Petals

Camille Petrocelli of Plantation, Fla., wrote about her serendipitous crafting experience when she was punching some small holes in a piece of paper. The punched-out pieces fell into the glue on her worktable and formed what to her looked like a small flower. Camille made her "accidental" flowers into earrings, and then turned her attention to making punched-paper flowers on purpose.

Materials

Card stock, greeting cards, magazine inserts, etc.

Scrap paper or extra card stock

Heart punch

Beads, glitter, glitter glue, etc. for flower centers

Scissors

Craft stick

Paper crimper (optional)

Yes! paste glue

Project note: *Experiment with different papers and different-shaped punches. On some of the flowers, I used smaller heart shapes in the center.*

1 With a craft stick, place a small mound of glue on a piece of scrap paper or card stock. After making one or two flowers, you will be able to determine the amount of glue you will need.

2 Punch out a number of heart-shaped pieces and crease each down the center. If desired, run pieces through a paper crimper.

3 Start by placing the pointed ends of the hearts into the glue and work around in a circle, overlapping each petal just a bit.

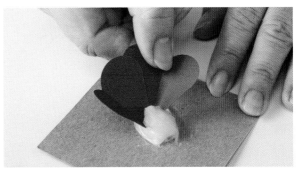

4 Keep adding petals until the flower pleases you. Add leaves if desired.

5 Cover the exposed glue with tiny beads, a single bead, glitter or glitter glue.

6 Allow to dry completely overnight and then cut away the bottom paper and embellish something with your flower! ∎

Note

The flowers that Camille sent to me were punched with heart-shaped punches from a variety of papers. Some were crimped. The flowers can be put on place cards, jewelry findings—anything that has a flat surface is fair game. Camille worked from the inside out, while I worked from the outside in. We agree that of the brands we tried, Yes! brand glue was the only one that worked for this project.

A Locking Letter

"Locking Letter"…That's the name that viewer Dee Harris of North Salem, Ind., gave to her idea for folding a piece of paper into thirds and making it stay that way. She sent along complete instructions, and I think it's not only rather a fun way to add a little variety to your letters, but a natural for printing out invitations either by hand or on your computer. She told us how to do that, too. Then, of course, we had to try a variation, but first, Dee's instructions and note.

Materials

- 8½ x 11-inch card stock or paper
- 2 designs or images— rubber stamped, cutouts from cards, stickers, photos, etc.
- Card stock (optional)
- Craft knife or scissors
- Fine-tip marker
- Ruler
- Pencil
- Bone folder (optional)
- Glue
- Computer and computer font (optional)

Note

To print computer-generated messages inside your letter, set your computer to landscape orientation, open the paper and type your message in the middle column only.

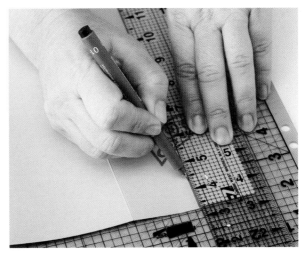

1 Score and fold an 8½ x 11 inch sheet of card stock or paper into thirds as if to put into a business-sized envelope. With the left side on top, draw, stamp or glue one design in lower center portion of the left panel.

2 Draw a line bisecting this flap. Use a ruler and jump over your design, continuing the line below.

3 Open up card stock and cut on the line and around the right side of your design. You might leave a little edge of card stock around the design.

4 Refold with the left panel still on top, and draw a line on the right panel along this cut edge.

5 Open the card stock, and draw, stamp or glue your second image or design to upper right side, making certain that it goes over the drawn line. Our images are stamped and embossed.

6 Open the card all the way. Cut on the drawn line going around the left side of the design.

7 Refold and lock the letter by having your designs overlap the center. Turn card over and crease over all with your hand or a bone folder to obtain clean, crisp folds. ∎

Another Option

To make the fold even more secure so that the letter really "locks" and lays flat, try this version.

1 Repeat steps 1–4 drawing the line in step 4 very faintly to use only as a guide for the placement of your second design. Repeat step 5. After drawing or gluing your design so that it bisects the line, erase the line and use your craft knife to cut along the outside left edge of your design.

2 When you refold the panels with the left panel on the top, the cut edge will slip under the cutout of the top design. Because the right panel was not cut off, the letter lays flat. We left ours slightly open for better visibility of the cuts and folds.

Bag 'Em

This idea for storing your rubber stamps is such a practical, logical and inexpensive solution that I couldn't resist including it in this book about paper, especially since all you card makers seem to be rubber stampers as well. All credit and thanks go to viewer RaLayne Lundburg. Because of her husband's career, RaLayne has to move frequently, and it was the packing and unpacking of all of her stamps each time that made her come up with this solution to her annoying problem. But you don't have to move often to think this is a good idea. I haven't moved in almost 30 years, and I now use it. No more "so many stamps, so little space." This tip not only saves space, but it is a wonderful way to locate specific stamps in a hurry.

Materials
2-gallon zip-top bags
12 x 15-inch pieces of
    sturdy cardboard
Cardboard or plastic
    storage carton
Permanent marking pen
Rubber stamps

1 Sort stamps as desired by subject, size, manufacturer, etc.

2 Arrange stamps on top of cardboard and insert into one of the plastic bags. Label the top of the bag.

3 Stand bags in the storage carton. The carton can be from the office-supply store, or a corrugated cardboard box you might cover with self-adhesive vinyl paper. ∎

Tip

I find it helpful to stamp the image on the cardboard in the spot I place the stamp. It makes it much easier to put the stamp back in the proper place when you return it after use.

Desktop Calendar

Viewer Nancy Sousa of Stonington, Conn., sent in a wonderful gift idea to make for anyone at anytime. It is inexpensive, personal, and something anyone can use. It's a small desktop calendar with every month of the year on a different card that you compose on your computer, print on your printer, stamp with your rubber stamps and slip into a clear acrylic frame. It is also versatile enough to go on a countertop, a dresser or on a bookcase. It's a winner!

Materials

4 x 6-inch stand-up acrylic frame*

Card stock for individual months

Rubber stamps, stickers, stencils, photographs, etc. for decorating

Computer and printer

Ink pad

Colored pencils or markers

Adhesive of choice

Colored card stock for layering images

Card stock for stamping images

Ruler

Craft knife

Cutting mat

The size and shape is optional. The frames are available with single or double photo spaces and are made to stand vertically or horizontally.

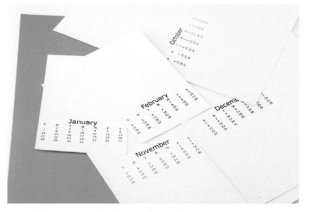

1 Choose a calendar style and stamp or print the months of the year based on the size of the frame. There are rubber stamps with month images, and a variety of calendars available on your computer in the various programs, as well as on search engines. I found mine by typing "calendar templates" into a search engine. Then I searched through the bunch until I found a suitable style for this project. Print out the 12 months, remembering to print them in the direction of the frame, and to allow space for decorating.

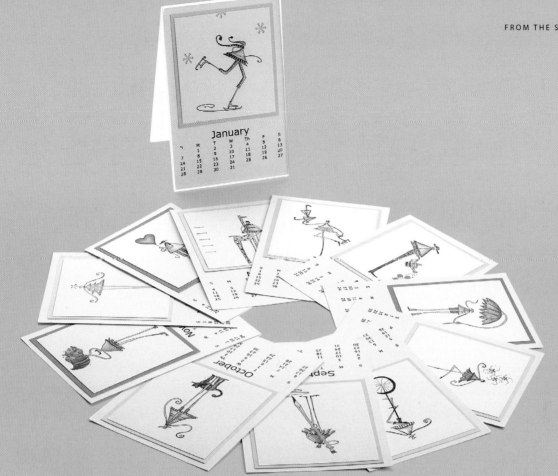

2 Cut out each month to fit the frame. Decorate each month as desired using rubber stamps, stickers, stencils or even photographs. Mat each stamped image onto coordinating card stock and attach to appropriate month. ■

Note

Nancy mentioned that she started making these calendars as Christmas gifts some years ago, and they have become very, very popular. Imagine being able to cut down on the "what shall I buy" problems each year! You can quickly make additional copies on a copy machine or make each set personalized for the recipient.

Molded Tissue Cards

If ever there was a card-making idea that should be in a book on paper crafting, this is it. Everything is paper. Several Christmases ago artist Julie Pearson of Traverse City, Mich., sent several of her beautiful holiday cards, and I was smitten immediately. I was stunned when she told me the molded designs were all made of toilet paper. I have since learned, of course, that the idea was not a new one, and it's not what you craft with, it's how you craft with it that makes the difference.

Materials

1-ply unprinted toilet tissue
Molds or rubber stamps
Window card
Card stock and printed papers (optional)
Items for embellishment such as gold pen, fine-tip black pen, glitter, rubber stamps, brads, etc.

Small stiff stencil brush
Adhesive of choice

Note: The mold you use should not be too dimensional. Julie often makes her own molds from polymer clay using earrings, pins and charms as items to mold. I have found that some rubber stamps work very well, as long as they are not too deep. Surprisingly, you don't need to make a mold. You can use them as they are. I experimented with any number of them. Some worked. Some didn't. All were fun to try.

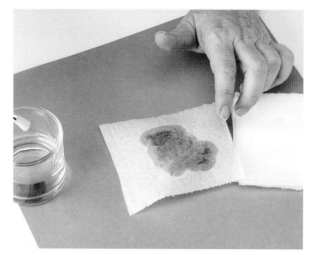

1 Place mold on work surface and cover with a single sheet of the 1-ply toilet tissue paper. Dip your brush in water and use it to dampen the paper and push it into the curves and crevices of the mold.

2 Place another sheet of the 1-ply tissue over the first and continue in the same manner. Continue until you have eight layers of the tissue. Allow to dry overnight.

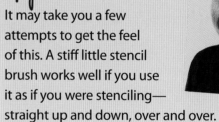

3 When the molded piece is completely dry, remove the paper from the mold and cut into a square slightly larger than window. Glue to piece of card stock cut slightly smaller than card and tape or glue card stock to back of card front. ■

Tip
It may take you a few attempts to get the feel of this. A stiff little stencil brush works well if you use it as if you were stenciling— straight up and down, over and over.

Card 1 Eight layers of the tissue were layered over a solid snowflake rubber stamp. When dry, it was removed from the stamp, cut into a square and glitter highlights were added with a glitter pen. It was then layered onto a piece of blue card stock cut slightly smaller than the size of the card front and was glued to the back side of the front of the card. A piece of snowflake-printed scrapbook paper was cut to a size slightly smaller than the front of the window card and a slightly larger window was cut in it. The piece was then layered to the front of the card. Inside, a strip of snowflake printed paper was placed down the right side and the message "Let it Snow! Let it Snow! Let it Snow!" was stamped on the inside.

Card 2 A rubber stamp was used as the mold (see page 167), but this was a much more detailed stamp than the snowflake and not as deep. When dry, the piece was cut into a square, and the prongs of a gold heart brad were poked through the paper heart. It was attached to the right-hand inside of a window card, so it would show through the window. A gold-leaf marker was used to add the border around the window. "Follow Your Dreams" is rubber stamped and embossed in gold below the window.

Card 3 This time the toilet tissue was layered over a flower-pattern rubber stamp. When dry, a pink-fluid chalk ink pad was rubbed over the flower, and a green-fluid chalk ink pad was rubbed over the stems and around the edge of the element. The cast was then glued to the right-hand inside of a window card, so it would show through the window. A pink window frame made from pink card stock was attached to the left-hand inside of the card and "i love you" was rubber stamped on the front.

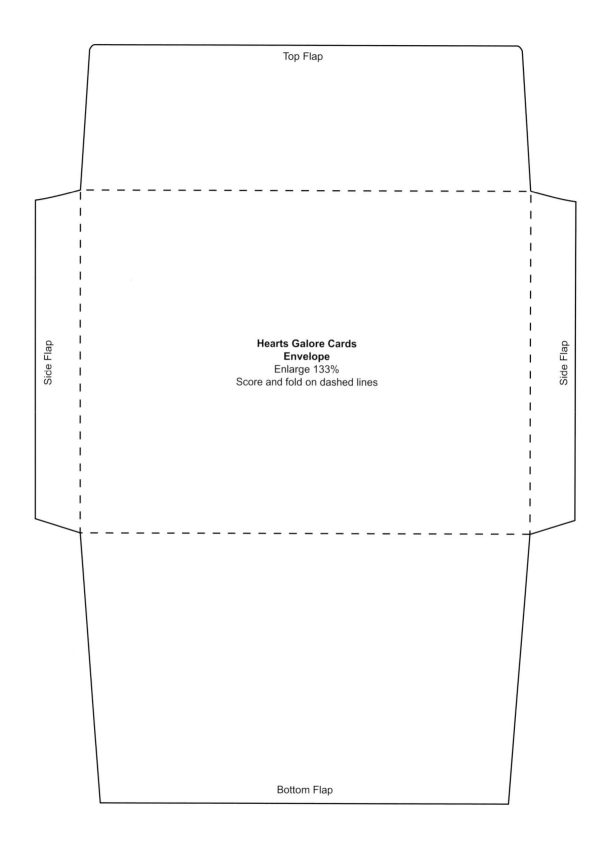

Top Flap

Side Flap

Hearts Galore Cards
Envelope
Enlarge 133%
Score and fold on dashed lines

Side Flap

Bottom Flap

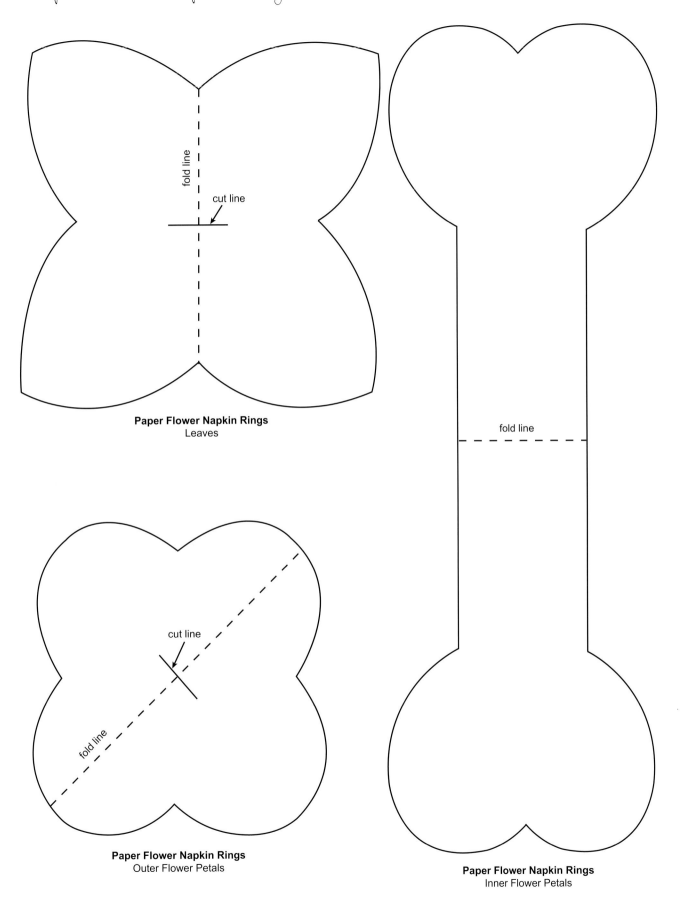

fold line

cut line

Paper Flower Napkin Rings
Leaves

cut line

fold line

Paper Flower Napkin Rings
Outer Flower Petals

fold line

Paper Flower Napkin Rings
Inner Flower Petals

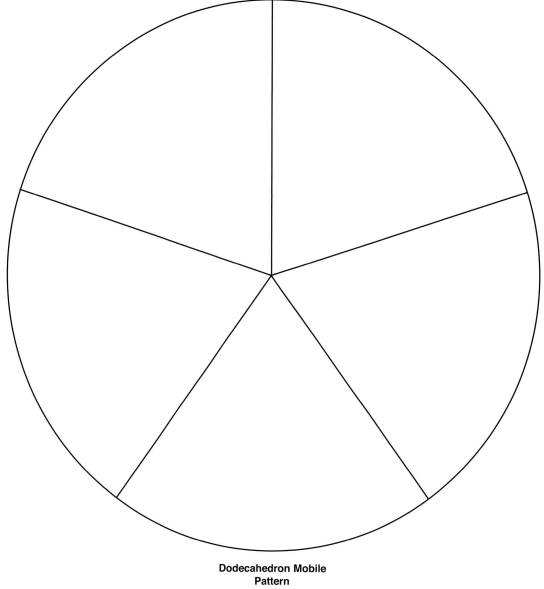

**Dodecahedron Mobile
Pattern**

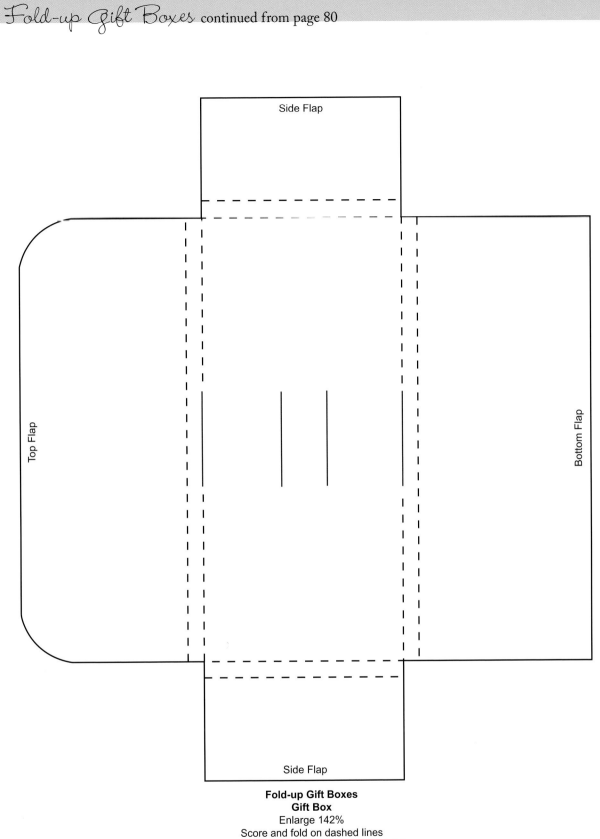

Fold-up Gift Boxes
Gift Box
Enlarge 142%
Score and fold on dashed lines
Optional: Cut on solid blue lines to insert ribbon.

BUYER'S GUIDE

Projects in this book were made using products provided by the manufacturers listed below. Look for the suggested products in your local craft- and art-supply stores. If unavailable, contact suppliers below. Some may be able to sell products directly to you; others may be able to refer you to retail sources.

CHALK TALK, page 9

Gift Package Rubber Stamp
KATIEBUG RUBBER STAMPS
www.katiebugstamps.com
(877) 724-1277

Alpha Stickers
ME & MY BIG IDEAS
www.meandmybigideas.com

Die-Cut Machine & Frog Die Cut
SIZZIX/ELLISION
www.sizzix.com
(949) 598-8822

WOVEN PAPER CARDS, page 12

Butterfly Rubber Stamp
MICHAEL STRONG RUBBER STAMPS
www.strongstamps.com
(619) 741-1836

Dragonflies Rubber Stamp
CUSTER'S LAST STAMP
www.custerslaststamp.com
(877) 908-1800

BLEACH PARTY, page 21

Butterfly Trio Rubber Stamp
INKADINKADO
stamp discontinued

Thank You Rubber Stamp
CLOSE TO MY HEART
www.closetomyheart.com
(888) 655-6552

Leaves Rubber Stamp
FRED B. MULLETT DESIGNS
www.fredbmullet.com
(206) 624-5723

Small Leaves Rubber Stamp
DELTA/RUBBER STAMPEDE
www.rubberstampede.com
(800) 423-4135

STAMPED POP-UP CARD, page 27

Trio Shadow Stamp, Butterfly & Dragonfly
POSH IMPRESSIONS through SUNDAY INTERNATIONAL
www.sundayint.com
(800) 401-8644

Thank You Rubber Stamp #A1920E
DELTA/RUBBER STAMPEDE
www.rubberstampede.com

Daisy Rubber Stamp #779H
THE ARTFUL STAMPER
www.artfulstamper.com

TWO-FOR-ONE CARDS, page 32

Cameo Frame Rubber Stamp
MUSEUM OF MODERN RUBBER
www.modernrubber.com

Checkered Frame Stamp
STAMPENDOUS
www.stampendous.com
(800) 869-0474

Markers
MARVY/UCHIDA
www.uchida.com
(800) 541-5877

Card Stock
DIE CUTS WITH A VIEW
www.dcwv.com
(801) 224-6766

ILLUMINATED LETTERS, page 37

L, O, V, E Rubber Stamps Gold Embossing Powder
JUDIKINS
www.judikins.com
(310) 515-1115

Embossing Ink
Clearsnap
www.clearsnap.com
(888) 448-4862

Embossing Heat Tool
MARVY/UCHIDA
www.uchida.com
(800) 541-5877

Permanent Markers— ZIG Pens
EK SUCCESS
www.eksuccess.com
(800) 524-1349

Colored Pencils
PRISMACOLOR
www.prismacolor.com
(800) 323-0749

Metallic Gold Leaf Pen
KRYLON/SHERWIN-WILLIAMS CO.
www.krylon.com
(800) 4krylon

POP-UP PACKAGES, page 54

Giftwrap
AMERICAN GREETINGS
www.americangreetings.com

ONE-SHEET MINI BOOKS, page 70

rob & bob Papers Die Cuts
PROVO CRAFT
www.provocraft.com
(800) 937-7686

Stickers
MRS. GROSSMAN'S PAPER CO.
www.mrsgrossmans.com
(800) 429-4549

Package Rubber Stamp
DE NAMI DESIGN
www.denamidesign.com
(253) 437-1626

FOLD-UP GIFT BOXES, page 80
Rubber Stamps
POSH IMPRESSIONS through
SUNDAY INTERNATIONAL
www.sundayint.com
(800) 401-8644

Ink Pads & Markers
MARVY/UCHIDA
www.uchida.com
(800) 541-5877

Adhesive-Backed Fabric
DELTA CREATIVE
www.deltacrafts.com
(800) 423-4135

MIZUHIKI DECORATED GIFT BOXES, page 88
Mizuhiki Cords
Red Liner Tape
YASUTOMO
www.yasutomo.com
(650) 737-8888

Lumiere Paints
JACQUARD PRODUCTS
RUPERT, GIBBON & SPIDER INC.
www.jacquardproducts.com
(707) 433-9577

Personal Die-Cut Machine & Dies
SIZZIX/ELLISON
www.sizzix.com
(877) 355-4766

QUOTES, FAMOUS & OTHERWISE, page 107
Rubber Stamps

MAGENTA RUBBER STAMPS
www.magentastyle.com
(450) 922-5253

Small Checkerboard Frame Rubber Stamp #536H
MARY ENGELBREIT
PLAID/ALL NIGHT MEDIA
www.allnightmedia.com

Checkerboard Frame Stamp
MARY ENGLEBREIT through
PLAID/ALL NIGHT MEDIA
www.allnightmedia.com
(800) 842-4197

Permanent Ink Pad
JUDIKINS
www.judikins.com
(310) 515-1115

Colored Pencils
PRISMACOLOR
www.prismacolor.com
(800) 323-0749

CLOCK IN A BAG, page 111
Clockworks
WALNUT HOLLOW
www.walnuthollow.com
(800) 950-5101

Handy Screw Punch
YASUTOMO
www.yasutomo.com
(650) 737-8888

REFRIGERATOR PUZZLES, page 115
Self-Stick Mounting Board
PRES-ON MOUNTING BOARDS
www.pres-on.com
(800) 323-1745

Laminating Sheet
CON-TACT Brand
(714) 736-1000

Self-Laminating Document Protectors
3M

www.scotchbrand.com
(888) 364-3577

NEVER-ENDING CARD, page 124
Thank You Rubber Stamp
JUDIKINS
www.judikins.com
(310) 515-1115

Daisy Rubber Stamp
CLUB SCRAP
www.clubscrap.com
(888) 634-9100

STAMP & FOLD FRAMES, page 128
Checkered Frame Stamp
POSH IMPRESSIONS through
SUNDAY INTERNATIONAL
www.sundayint.com
(500) 401-8644

Embossing Ink
CLEARSNAP
www.clearsnap.com
(888) 448-4862

Gold Embossing Powder
JUDIKINS
www.judikins.com
(310) 515-1115

Embossing Heat Tool
MARVY/UCHIDA
www.uchida.com
(800) 541-5877

LOOK WHO'S TALKING, page 131
Laminate/Magnet Machine & Cartridge (optional)
XYRON
www.xyron.com
(800) 793-3523

Laminating Sheets
Self-Laminating Document Protectors
3M
www.scotchbrand.com
(888) 364-3577

PERSONALITY FRAMES, page 137

Adhesive—Bookbinding Glue
CLUB SCRAP
www.clubscrap.com
(888) 634-9100

JACOB'S LADDER PHOTO HOLDER, page 140

Papers
Ribbons
Mat Board
CLUB SCRAP
www.clubscrap.com
(888) 634-9100

"LEFTOVERS" CARDS, page 141

Butterfly Rubber Stamp
MICHAEL STRONG RUBBER STAMPS
www.strongstamps.com
(619) 741-1836

Embossing Ink
Embossing Powder
Embossing Heat Tool
RANGER INDUSTRIES
www.rangerink.com
(732) 389-3535

PHOTO MOSAIC CARDS, page 149

Focal Point Stamp
MAGENTA RUBBER STAMPS
www.magentastyle.com
(450) 922-5253

CRAFTING WITH ENVELOPE LININGS, page 153

Die-Cut Machine & Dies
SIZZIX/ELLISON
www.sizzix.com
(877) 355-4766

Rubber Stamps
Embossing Powder
JUDIKINS
www.judikins.com
(310) 515-1115

Rubber Stamp Sayings
Unknown Source

PUNCHED PAPER PETALS, page 156

YES! Paste
GANE BROTHERS & LANE INC.
www.ganebrothers.com
(800) 323-0596

Stickles Glitter Glue
RANGER INDUSTRIES
www.rangerink.com
(732) 389-3535

Heart Punches—various sizes
MARVY/UCHIDA
www.uchida.com
(800) 541-5877

A LOCKING LETTER, page 158

Stickers
ME & MY BIG IDEAS
www.meandmybigideas.com

Swirl Heart Open Rubber Stamp #A2106E
DELTA/RUBBER STAMPEDE
www.rubberstampede.com
(800) 423-4135

Embossing Ink
Embossing Powder
Embossing Heat Tool
RANGER INDUSTRIES
www.rangerink.com
(732) 389-3535

BAG 'EM, page 162

Two-Gallon Storage Bags
ZIPLOC
www.ziploc.com
(800) 494-4855

DESKTOP CALENDAR, page 164

Rubber Stamps
AMERICAN ART STAMP
www.americanartstamp.com
(310) 371-6593

Umbrellas Rubber Stamp
MAGENTA RUBBER STAMPS
www.magentastyle.com
(450) 922-5253

Cornucopia Rubber Stamp
Unknown Source

Permanent Ink Pad
JUDIKINS
www.judikins.com
(310) 515-1115

Colored Pencils
PRISMACOLOR
www.prismacolor.com
(800) 323-0749

Background Scrapbook Papers
DIE CUTS WITH A VIEW
www.dcwv.com
(801) 224-6766

MOLDED TISSUE CARDS, page 167

Heart Rubber Stamp
Cynthia Hart's Scrapbooking Stamp Collection #203705
DELTA/RUBBER STAMPEDE
www.rubberstampede.com
(800) 423-4135

Snowflake Rubber Stamp
MUSEUM OF MODERN RUBBER
stamp discontinued

Flower Rubber Stamp
RUBBER MOON
www.rubbermoon.com

Cat's Eyes Fluid Chalk Ink Pads
CLEARSNAP
www.clearsnap.com
(888) 448-4862